NORVELL

ASTROLOGY
ROMANCE, YOU AND THE STARS

NORVELL

Your Star-Guide to Happiness
How Astrology Can Help You Win
Love, Wealth and Fame

Melvin Powers
Wilshire Book Company

12015 Sherman Road, No. Hollywood, CA 91605

MANUFACTURED IN THE UNITED STATES OF AMERICA

ISBN 0-87980-011-9

CONTENTS

SIGNS OF ZODIAC

Aries - - - - - - - *March 21 to April 20*

Taurus - - - - - - - *April 21 to May 20*

Gemini - - - - - - - *May 21 to June 20*

Cancer - - - - - - - *June 21 to July 22*

Leo - - - - - - - - *July 23 to Aug. 22*

Virgo - - - - - - - *Aug. 23 to Sept. 22*

Libra - - - - - - - *Sept. 23 to Oct. 22*

Scorpio - - - - - - *Oct. 23 to Nov. 22*

Sagittarius - - - - - *Nov. 23 to Dec. 21*

Capricorn - - - - - - *Dec. 22 to Jan. 19*

Aquarius - - - - - - *Jan. 20 to Feb. 19*

Pisces - - - - - - - *Feb. 20 to March 20*

★ 1 ★

WHAT ASTROLOGY CAN DO
FOR YOUR LIFE

YOU are walking along a road in a strange open country. You come to a fork in the road, and you stop, at a loss to know which turning leads to your goal. Suddenly you see a signpost standing there, and now the way lies clear ahead.

Note this well. The signpost points the right road. *But you must travel it with your own efforts.* The signpost cannot help you.

Astrology is the signpost of human life and endeavor. It points your true path. But Astrology is not a free ticket to your harbor of happiness—*you must travel the road yourself.*

To reach your goal in life, you must follow the plain guides to your destiny. In this book, I propose to point out these guides to you. To make use of them and fulfill your destiny, there are a great many practical things which you must know and do.

I will tell you these things.

Astrology, the science of learning man's character

and destiny through a study of the governing forces radiating from the planetary bodies, is one of the oldest of the sciences. In the very fact that Astrology has come down through the centuries unchanged except for the addition of new knowledge lies the gre proof of its verity and force.

Learned geographers once believed that the world was flat . . . but the science of Astrology has survived the challenge of the centuries. Learned doctors once taught that disease was caused by some strange miasma rising from the earth . . . but the science of Astrology remains today the unaltered teachings of the Ancients.

Through the ages men of learning have sought for truth, and many a "science" has fallen before their attacks. *If Astrology were not truth, it could not have survived.*

The radiations of the planets—of which the sun, of course, is one—have an obvious effect on plant and animal life. A plant bathed in the emanations of the sun blooms and thrives. A man, even a very giant of a man, hidden from the sun in a dungeon becomes in time a dwarfed, diseased, and mentally deformed thing. The direct effect of the moon on the tides, and on the periods of women, is a known fact.

Going a step further, the radiations of the planets have an equally clear effect upon the emotions, the spirits of a man. You yourself are cheered and uplifted in the presence of the sun, depressed in its absence. You are romantic under the influence of the moon, and serene in the peace of the stars.

Your "character" is a combination of abilities, tendencies, traits, and emotions. Your emotions are part and parcel of your character. The radiations of the planets have a provable effect not only upon your emotions, but upon your *whole* character—shaping your character at birth, and moulding your destiny throughout your whole life.

It is startling to see present day physicists and astronomers, by nature and training so skeptical of anything they cannot picture or hold in their hands, beginning to admit the existence and dynamic power of these "unknown" forces. Cosmic Rays; vast and powerful magnetic fields beyond our earthly atmosphere; the effect of sun spots on radio reception; such things as these lead cold, dispassionate scientists to admit that they are treading on the edge of the Unknown.

Such a savant as Dr. W. J. Humphries (Physicist of the U. S. Weather Bureau, and chairman of the sage American Geophysical Union) says, "Our earth is in the midst of gravity fields, electrical fields, and magnetic fields. It is bombarded by electrons and alpha particles shot out of the sun, and perhaps out of the stars as well. The cosmic rays, whose exact nature is not yet known, bombard the earth from outer space. *Undoubtedly there are other radiations which we have not yet tracked down.*" The Minneapolis Journal adds this comment on his remarks: "Perhaps some of the sages and wise men of ancient times, in their long black robes and conical hats, who used the word Astrology very freely, knew more about the kind of influence exerted by other members of the solar system than they have been given credit for." Truly, there are great influences which lie beyond the narrow realm of test-tubes and telescopes.

Nevertheless, it must be admitted that modern Astrology owes much to these same test-tubes and telescopes. In primitive civilizations men worshipped the sun, the moon, and the stars. This was blind worship: these peoples simply *felt* the influences exerted on their lives, with no idea of the why and the how. Modern Astrology owes a debt to that first great thinker who noted and pondered upon the fact that when certain planets went through certain transits, and when the Sun and Moon passed through certain phases, corresponding changes were noted in the affairs of men. That discovery sounded the knell of superstition and ignorance. Modern Astrology owes only a slightly lesser debt to the scientists and their instruments of the recent centuries, because their research into the movements of the planets and relationships to each other, has made possible the refinement and amazing accuracy of Astrology today. But the greatest debt of all is owed to religion, with which Astrology marches hand in hand. The teachings of the great religious leaders and philosophers gave to the ancient Astrologers the true pattern and purpose of man's life on earth; laying bare those things of the spirit, the soul, and the destiny, toward which the Astrologers had been groping. Astrology pays this debt in small part by making scientifically demonstrable the teachings of religion. Jesus said, "Know thyself"—we say, "Your destiny lies hidden within your own character." Jesus said, "Love ye one another"—we say, "Learn the influences at work in the lives of your friends, that you may better work in harmony with them." Jesus said, "Seek ye the kingdom of Heaven"—and we say, "Conduct your life in harmony with the currents of the Universe, to develop yourself to spiritual perfection."

Man, as Jesus taught, is a weak and insignificant instrumentality of an omnipotent destiny. In the earthly time allotted us before we pass to the Great Hereafter, we want desperately to develop within ourselves a state of spiritual perfection; to cope with the problems which constantly arise about us; to find happiness in our lives on earth. To these worthy ends, Astrology is a fitting and awe-inspiring instrument provided for us to use, and to control.

YOU AND THE STARS

It is unfortunate that Astrology is sometimes practiced by those who do not regard it as a sacred trust. Medicine has its quacks. The Law has its shysters. We too are cursed with malpractitioners who drag the honest uses of Astrology in the dust by claiming impossible things for it.

I have already told you that Astrology presents you with no free ticket to success and happiness: that though it points out the road, you must follow that road yourself. I want to go further.

You were born under a certain set of planetary influences. As we know, these influences have had a tremendous effect in shaping and moulding that set of abilities, potentialities, leanings, predilections, traits and emotions which we call your character. We know that a person born when the Sun was in a certain relationship to the other planets will *in all likelihood* have certain marked characteristics, weaknesses, business or artistic abilities, faults, susceptibility to diseases, and so on.

But when a pseudo-Astrologer takes a certain individual and states flatly that certain things are absolutely and finally true, without possibility of argument, that man is violating his trust.

Would you like to confound this man? Then ask him this question: "Of two people born at precisely the same moment of time, could not one conceivably become President and the other a pauper?" Of course such a thing could happen. Because the radiations of the planets, though undoubtedly the most powerful influence, are but one of several which mould the individual character and shape the destiny. Heredity is one of these: who can dispute that a child inherits the strength and weakness, the intellectual capacity of its parents? Environment is another: who doubts that a farm boy will develop differently from a youngster brought up in the slums? Still another is Education.

Certain capacities, certain limitations are placed on each individual before and after his birth. True it is that an individual will react to the planetary stimuli he absorbed at the moment of his birth, but only to the extent that his inherited body and brain react, and no more. The true science of Astrology teaches that the qualities we possess are enhanced or modified by the planets, but not completely changed or ever set aside at any time in our lives.

The results of this betrayal can be tragic. The pseudo-Astrologer, in his anxiety to please or amaze, misses the light of hope for the individual which lies in one vital truth. Regardless of accidents of heredity, environment or education, the mark of the planetary influences, even though submerged, *always remains*. Any individual has within himself, therefore, the priceless power to rise above his limitations and thereby fulfill his destiny. If he but learn his hidden reserves of character, and doggedly pursue the path set for him in the heavens, he can overcome his earthly obstacles and forge the way to his goals.

Theodore Roosevelt was a weak and puny child. He was, however, born under the sign of Scorpio, which had implanted in him the latent promise of a healthy, strong body. He triumphed over his earthly handicap, as we know, and fulfilled the promise of his destiny by emerging as the American symbol of all that is physically vigorous and dynamic.

You, if you know your own destiny and latent powers, can surmount your own earthly disadvantages. Conversely, you can, by your own efforts, also rise above any handicaps with which your stars may have burdened you. But in either case, you must *know* your destiny and you must know it in full: the bitter with the sweet.

It is with this in mind that I intend to break away from the gush, the wordy vagueness, confusing technicality, and meaningless flattery with which Astrology has too often been treated in books. I am going to tell you some unpleasant things about yourself. I am going to warn you of possible misfortune, failure and tragedy. I am going to strip the veil from certain of your tendencies which you would perhaps prefer not to admit even to yourself.

When I displease you, forgive me, for I am warning you of these things for your own good. When I indicate a possible misfortune, or probe a weakness in your character, remember that forewarned is forearmed. And if I cite your lack of ability for a certain pursuit, I do so with the sincere belief that you will best reach success by concentrating your powers upon the things your destiny has decreed for you, avoiding waste effort. For just as your destiny can overcome earthly handicaps, so your earthly efforts can overcome certain handicaps with which your destiny has burdened you. But to achieve your triumph, you must know the truth: not merely the pleasant and flattering truth, but the *whole* truth.

It is my duty to give it to you.

HOW TO USE THIS BOOK

By probing your hidden character, you can capitalize your abilities and overcome your weaknesses.

By knowing when the planetary radiations are positive and good, or negative and bad, you can conduct your affairs and human relationships in harmony with the birthpath which the stars have set for you.

By gaining an insight into the hidden character of other persons and their probable reactions to you, you achieve the power to attract others, to encourage relationships which are desirable and to avoid those which are destined to end unhappily.

The Sun passes through the twelve signs of the Zodiac at approximately the same time each year. You, and every other person now living, belong to one of these signs. If I were building a complete personal Horoscope for you I would have to know as closely as possible the exact minute and year of your birth, but the Sun, being the most powerful of the nine Planets in our solar system, has the greatest effect upon the things with which we are here concerned: namely, character, and that broad line of destiny which has its roots in character.

I will not burden you with the involved technical side of the subject. This book has been constructed so that you need to know only one thing: the sign of the Zodiac under which you were born, or the sign of the person whom you wish to know more about. These signs, which depend simply upon the date of birth, are listed hereafter.

It should be mentioned that the Sun passes gradually, rather than abruptly, from one sign to another. This period of transition, known as the Cusp of a sign, lasts for the six or seven days from about the 17th to the 23rd of each month. If your birthdate happens to fall in this Cusp period, you will show influences of the adjacent sign as well as your own.

Thus, if you were born on the 19th day of May, when the Sun was about to transit from Taurus to Gemini, you would fall nominally into the sign of Taurus. Logically, however, you would naturally partake also of rather strong Gemini influences, and you should therefore consider the influences of both signs, reading both sections.

The first chapter, entitled "YOUR TRUE CHARACTER," analyzes the traits with which the planetary influences blessed or burdened you at birth. In this chapter is your guide to the abilities which you should stress, and the weaknesses against which you should stand constant guard. For insight into the character, the likes and dislikes, and the potentials of another person with whom you may be entering a relationship, read what is written in this chapter under that person's sign.

The other chapters discuss each of the twelve signs in relation to one major human goal. For guidance in a certain problem, simply turn to the chapter which relates to it and read what is set forth in the section headed by the proper sign.

As an example, let us suppose you are considering embarking on a business venture. You were born, we'll say, on November 10th, which is in the sign of Scorpio. Turn to the chapter on "BUSINESS AND FINANCES," and under the heading "SCORPIO" you will find that (subject always to outside influences of heredity, environment and education) you tend to conduct yourself in certain ways, are fitted or unfitted to this particular type of business, possess or lack the specific qualities which this enterprise demands.

Continuing this example, let us suppose that the proposed venture is to be a partnership. Your contemplated partner was born on April 6th (the particular year, in this analysis of the effect of the constant *Sun*, does not matter), which is Aries. In the same chapter, study the Aries section for information on his business abilities and hidden character: conclude whether you and he are apt to get on well together, or whether you will tend to clash.

A question of romance or marriage should be approached in the same fashion. Study yourself under your sign in the proper chapters, then study the person with whom you are in love. But may I caution you, on these matters, to consider the matter with your head rather than your heart.

FIND YOUR BIRTHSIGN FROM THIS TABLE

begins   ends

March 22–April 20 ARIES: A fire sign, ruled by Mars. Symbol, the Ram.

April 21–May 20 TAURUS: An earth sign, ruled by Venus. Symbol, the Bull.

May 21–June 20	GEMINI: An air sign, ruled by Mercury. Symbol, the Twins.
June 21–July 22	CANCER: A water sign, ruled by Moon. Symbol, the Crab.
July 23–August 22	LEO: A fire sign, ruled by Sun. Symbol, the Lion.
August 23–Sept. 22	VIRGO: An earth sign, ruled by Mercury. Symbol, the Virgin.
Sept. 23–Oct. 22	LIBRA: An air sign, ruled by Venus. Symbol, the Scales.
Oct. 23–Nov. 22	SCORPIO: A water sign, ruled by Mars. Symbol, the Scorpion.
Nov. 23–Dec. 21	SAGITTARIUS: A fire sign, ruled by Jupiter. Symbol, the Archer.
Dec. 22–Jan. 19	CAPRICORN: An earth sign, ruled by Saturn. Symbol, the Goat.
Jan. 20–Feb. 18	AQUARIUS: An air sign, ruled by Uranus. Symbol, Water-Bearer.
Feb. 19–March 20	PISCES: A water sign, ruled by Neptune. Symbol, the Fishes.

★ 2 ★

YOUR TRUE CHARACTER

BE honest with yourself.

I can do you no good if you beam with pleasure at the nice things I say about you, only to hide your head in the sand and refuse to admit, even to yourself, the existence of undesirable qualities. Yet we all have them. I say to you that a bad tendency with which you were born can be overcome only if you search yourself and admit that such a tendency exists.

The Sun was in a certain position, or Sign, at the moment of your birth. The Sun, being the most powerful of the ruling Planets, exerted a tremendous force on the formation of your character. These inborn characteristics, and the destiny which flows inevitably from them, remain implanted within you until you die, submerged though they may be for the moment by the other forces of heredity, education and environment. A submerged characteristic or power can be released from its bondage if you will recognize

14

its latent presence and bend your efforts to its development.

To better understand your true character, your hidden powers, your life pattern and eventual destiny, study that section in the following pages which deals with your Sign. Learn from it your birthright of traits, powers, abilities, and emotional tendencies, to the end that you may discover and work in harmony with the forces which are guiding your life. Then with this new knowledge of your true self, go on to the other chapters which deal with the various departments of your life and your desires.

But—be honest with yourself.

ARIES

(Mar. 22–Apr. 20)

Born when the Sun was in the first sign of the Zodiac, you absorbed the powerful vibrations of the Sun and your ruling planet, Mars. This sign, the leader in the Zodiac, represents the head and brains: the intellectual and reasoning faculties.

Your outstanding trait is that of determination. Your aggressiveness, coupled with your unusual mental equipment, fits you for leadership in either business or artistic pursuits. You have also the power to attract influential friends, and a strong liking for social life: added assets in your climb to the top.

Mars, your ruling planet, gives you great courage in the face of ostacles, and contributes to your determination and forcefulness. There is nothing you cannot do in life if you apply these powers constructively, *but you have the capacity within you to twist these powers to harmful ends.* Mars inclines you to rash, impulsive decisions at times, makes you somewhat reckless and inclined to hasty action before proper thought. Unless you guard against these tendencies you will find friction, misunderstanding, and dispute arising in all departments of your life. So before you embark on a course of action, and especially before you sign leases, contracts, and other important papers, think things over carefully by yourself, secure the advice of friends who have your interests at heart, and *take your time.* Try to avoid making decisions under pressure.

This becomes doubly important because you are high-minded and idealistic, sympathetic and trusting. This trustfulness makes you easily deceived, and your sympathy permits others to impose upon you. You must learn to distinguish flattery from honest praise, and cultivate more firmness in dealing with people, even though it sometimes hurts.

Your chances for success in life are excellent. Though your aggressiveness inclines you to a business career, money means to you not so much dollars and cents as a symbol of security and power. Early in life you may experience confusion and reverses through being misguided or started on the wrong course. But once you find yourself, everything indicates that you will forge ahead with unusual rapidity. Early responsibilities are the rule with Aries, and this training will stand you in good stead for the future. Some early training along creative or artistic lines is also desirable to balance the commercial side of your nature.

Your nature responds best to kindness, and you resent the use of arbitrary force. You resent criticism, and must fight a tendency to resent even suggestion. However, your intelligence is great enough to permit you to sweep aside your instinctive resentment and accept criticism, especially if it is constructive and offered in an honestly friendly and helpful spirit. You must guard against this tendency to resent and reject criticism, because your aggressiveness makes it necessary that your actions be well-considered and sometimes curbed.

Emotionally, you are on the whole well balanced. There is a tendency toward moodiness; you are inclined to be impressionable and temperamental. Others can easily depress or elate your spirits. You are highly imaginative; being affectionate, sincere and generous, you are willing to go to great lengths to help a friend. You are, as I say, a good friend, but once you turn against someone you are finished for all time. Make certain you have due provocation before ejecting a friend from your life.

Aries gives you the power to take your place in the highest circles of business and social life. More than one important person will assist you in your climb to fame and fortune, probably a person in the law, medicine, politics or banking circles—perhaps a figure in the creative arts.

Your destiny under Aries can well be a position of leadership and trust in government or public life.

A study of the lives of certain famous persons born under your sign of Aries, and partaking of the same influences, may be of value to you: Presidents John Tyler and Thomas Jefferson; Statesmen Sir Neville Chamberlain and Henry Clay; Authors William Wordsworth and Washington Irving; Businessmen J. Pierpont Morgan and Charles Schwab; Actors Spencer Tracy, Mary Pickford, Charles Chaplin, Gloria Swanson and Bette Davis.

TAURUS

(Apr. 21–May 20)

Taurus is the second sign of the Zodiac, ruling wealth and things of the earth. Investments or pursuits connected with the earth, such as real estate, horticulture, lumber, mining, oil, and agriculture, are favored for Taurus-born. It is generally through investments of this nature that Taurus fortunes are made.

But you also absorbed the creative and artistic vibrations of your ruling planet Venus at the time of your birth, and as a result your nature is a strange mixture of the commercial and artistic. This is further complicated by the fact that Taurus rules the throat, tongue and vocal cords (many famous singers and actors were born in this sign), so that your inborn fluency of speech, wit and conversational brilliance also inclines you to the artistic side.

The result is that you are apt to find your interests strangely divided throughout life, your ambitions and activities constantly swaying between the commercial and artistic. This divided mind is apt to prove your downfall and you must guard against it. Early training is desirable for you, so that you may find the right occupation before it is too late.

You were born while the Sun's energy was stimulating and awakening all life in the early Spring. This stimulation has made you mentally alert and emotionally intense, given to constant activity and motion. You like change, and actually welcome beginning a new project or moving to a new location; your constructive, active and creative mind gets many ideas for stories, songs, inventions and so on which might make you a fortune *if you followed them through.* There is your pitfall. The very activity of your mind makes you whimsical and inclined to drop one thing for something new, finding it difficult to sustain your interest.

Success to you means money and the things that money will buy. You want and enjoy to the full the luxuries of life: the comfortable homes, clothes, and cars. You are both acquisitive and possessive, delighting in accumulating plenty of this world's goods. But fortunately you balance this acquisitiveness with unusual generosity—though this characteristic can betray you through your susceptibility to flattery. As a matter of fact, you are apt to be too generous for your own good, and you must keep a rein on this tendency lest you be dominated by others and unfairly burdened with their responsibilities. Watch out also for your inclination to husband your money over a long period only to scatter it all in one wild splurge. Your best safeguard is a plan of consistent saving, investment on a basis of reason, and refusal to put all your financial eggs in one basket. This is not easy for you to do.

You will find yourself subject to "hunches," guided at times by a psychic or intuitive inner voice. You should listen to this. Your first decision, unlike that of an Aries subject, is apt to be correct. Long deliberation, especially if you listen to the over-persuasion of others, tends to muddle you and subject you to vacillation between one opinion and the other. You are naturally a shrewd appraiser of persons, and your quick judgment is usually accurate. When you act on your own first wishes you are strong-minded and decisive; acting on these will usually save you later mistakes.

This power of quick decision inclines you to be positive and strong-willed—qualities which you must not permit to degenerate into their first cousins, obstinacy and stubbornness. Since you like to, and can, control the lives of others, you should seek your place in executive work or in positions dealing with the public where these qualities can be recognized and utilized. If you can only learn to choose your best line and then follow it without shifting at every alluring prospect which comes along, your chances for financial success are better than average.

Your best chance probably lies in artistic or creative work. Nevertheless, the struggle between your commercial and artistic leanings is going to be a severe one. If after considering and discarding your prospects in art, acting, writing or music, you take up a commercial career, you should most certainly follow some creative hobby or avocation which gives release to the strong artistic side of your nature.

Emotionally, Venus is your ruler. The sex impulse of Taurus is strongly developed. You are over-emotional, and very affectionate. But you complicate this by being undemonstrative in public, which sometimes leads to misunderstanding by your loved ones. Your great weakness, I must warn you, is in romance, and unless you use the greatest caution in managing this side of your life, you are destined to suffer several bitter heartaches. These will arise from your emotional nature, and from the fact that you are sensitive, romantic—and somewhat fickle. Do not permit your emotional nature to get the best of you, for this will dissipate your energies. If transmuted, however, this great emotional energy can carry you to great heights.

A study of the lives of these famous persons, also born under the sign of Taurus, may be of value to you: Presidents James Buchanan and James Monroe; Authors Marie Corelli, Herbert Spencer, and Dante; Soldier the Duke of Wellington; Explorer Peary; Publisher Hearst; Dictator Hitler; Singers and Actors Mme. Melba, Tyrone Power, Shirley Temple, Margaret Sullavan, Bing Crosby, Alice Faye, Gary Cooper.

GEMINI

(May 21–June 20)

Gemini is the third sign in the Zodiac, ruled by the mental planet Mercury.

YOUR TRUE CHARACTER

Your symbol is the Twins, and therein lies the clue to the strange duality of this sign. Mercury bestowed upon you a strong and brilliant mind. But the Twins burden you with the curse of indecision. You have within you the power to rise to the pinnacles of fame and happiness, or to sink to the depths, depending upon how well you gain control of your tendency to waste and scatter your talents and vacillate between two courses in life. You seem always to stand at the crossroads of indecision in romance, business, friendship, occupation, and even in travel. If you can gain the ascendancy over this inclination to be torn between two courses, blending the two halves of your mind into one perfect whole, you have it within you to go further than almost any other sign.

This duality carries through to your human relationships. You are socially inclined and can be extraordinarily charming—when you choose. You make friends quickly—but cast them aside for new friends just as quickly when your interest wanes. You can be witty, agreeable and vitally interesting, and you delight in conversing with those you like at the moment. But unless your interest is instantly captured you are inclined to set up a barrier which makes you difficult to understand. You like rather too well being the center of any group; you judge rather harshly and quickly, find fault and criticize others too readily without taking the trouble to inquire into their motives. In short, you have within yourself the power to move in the highest social circles—or to be friendless and alone, depending upon how well you recognize and develop the positive qualities of your sign. But this strange duality carries with it a great power. You are blessed with amazing versatility. Your strangely adaptable nature makes you capable of moulding yourself successfully to almost any destiny you may choose.

As a result of this, plus your equipment for mental work, your chances for success are very pronounced, once you overcome your tendency to indecision. You are personable and can meet the public; you are able to apply yourself diligently to the matter in hand, and your mind is so alert and rapid that you comprehend instantly complicated matters and situations which others must study at length.

But you are impatient of restraint and impulsive, often so anxious to leap ahead to your goal that you neglect the necessary preliminary groundwork. You must take the necessary time for personal development and study before you can expect to take your place at the top.

Most Gemini subjects who achieve power and fortune have done so through their aptitude for friendship, shrewdly choosing those persons who can help them most in their pursuits. You will probably attach yourself early to some important person and rise with him; or as an alternative, get into some field where your mental abilities will be recognized and carry you to success.

In view of the fact that your reactions and interests are mental rather than physical, it is surprising to find that your emotional nature is volatile, tempestuous, and inclined to be rather unrestrained. You are restless and anxious to change about from place to place and person to person, a handicap if indulged to the point where you let vital opportunities slip through your fingers through want of following through.

More than any other sign of the Zodiac, unhappiness can come to you through *your own actions* in romance. You love deeply when and while you love, but when you have occasion to forget a person, you do so completely. You are inclined to be flirtatious to the point where members of the opposite sex are driven to desperation by your capriciousness. Your sex impulses must be directed with utmost care into channels that are constructive. You are a good friend, but a bad enemy; left to themselves, your affections vacillate. Concentration upon the training of your excellent mind, especially in the arts and literature, will help you control your pitfalls of vacillation and indecision.

YOU AND THE STARS

I suggest you study, with these things in mind, the lives of these famous persons born under the same set of influences: Authors Sir Arthur Conan Doyle, Julia Ward Howe, Walt Whitman, and Ralph Waldo Emerson; Statesmen Patrick Henry, Jefferson Davis; Soldiers Nathan Hale and Nathaniel Greene; Composer Richard Wagner; Artist Paul Rembrandt; Pope Pius X; Brigham Young, and William Rockefeller.

CANCER

(June 21–July 22)

Cancer is the fourth sign of the Zodiac. At the time of your birth you were ruled by the changeable and fickle Moon.

The Moon gives you a strange sub-surface nature. Representing as it does the secret forces of life, subjects born under its domination are intuitive, mysterious, and attracted toward the Occult. You are able to keep a secret, and you enjoy doing so—to such an extent, in fact, that there is probably a hidden chapter in your life which is unconfided even to your most intimate friend. You progress better when you carry out your various projects cloaked in a veil of secrecy. Mysterious and unusual happenings are apt to come into your life when the Moon is in the full, or in the dark of the Moon. Your best time to begin new projects and meet new friends is when the moon is in the first quarter.

You are very apt to have an inferiority complex, to shrink from meeting people, suffering from self-consciousness and lack of confidence. This complex is unjustified. It rises from your tendency to live within yourself, plus your inclination to be sensitive, easily hurt, and impressionable. But you were given a beautiful mind, with unusual qualities, and you can be very personable and attractive when you force yourself to come out of your shell. Once you know these reasons for your feelings of shyness and inferiority you can overcome them. You should most certainly try, for your shrinking from people can easily become a phobia which will cause you much misery.

Your nature is domestic and sentimental. A beautiful home environment means a great deal to you, and you devote much of your hope and thought to creating it. You like beautiful objects, soft music, and a peaceful environment. Quarrelling, discord and confusion cause you more pain than the other signs. You seek constantly the beautiful and good in people, but tend to retire into your shell when others intrude on your privacy. Though you dream of bold deeds, your outward bearing and nature is characterized by shyness and modesty. However, when your happiness or security is threatened, you rise to supreme heights of courage and daring, your temper becomes explosive, and your natural softness takes on firmness and determination.

Your love for beautiful things leads to extravagance, a tendency which, especially in women, must be strictly controlled lest it get out of hand. You should recognize and admit that money is important to your future happiness, for you must have your share of the good and beautiful things of life. This item must, I fear, be considered in choosing a husband, for it will be very difficult for a Cancer woman to be happy with a failure.

Romance and marriage mean a great deal to you. You are especially fond of members of the opposite sex, though your inclination is to be somewhat flirtatious. Your power in romantic matters must not be abused, for carelessness on your part is quite apt to cause broken hearts.

Your sign is distinctive and apt to go far in life. Your success, however, is apt to be unheralded, because your logical place is in a position of trust or power behind the scenes rather than that of the extroverted person who works and mixes with the world. You are poetic and creative, and will probably turn to writing, music or painting at least as a relaxation or hobby. This creative side of your mind fits you for work requiring inspirational ideas. The highly developed spiritual side of the Cancer nature, in conjunction with its creativeness and tendency to the mystic, has brought forth many leaders in philosophy and religion.

Financial success, which is quite apt to come to you if that inferiority complex can be overcome, will probably be accompanied by philanthropies of a civic nature, directed toward the betterment of mankind as a whole, rather than to individuals.

Note well these famous persons born in your sign, and let their lives guide you in your own problems: Presidents John Quincy Adams and Calvin Coolidge; Creators Rubens, Sir Joshua Reynolds, Nathaniel Hawthorne, Jean Jacques Rousseau; men of business, John D. Rockefeller, Stuyvesant Fish, John Wanamaker; the founder of Christian Science, Mary Baker Eddy; Actors Irene Dunne, Ginger Rogers, Barbara Stanwyck, and Andrea Leeds.

LEO

(July 23–Aug. 22)

Ruled by the powerful Sun, Leo is known as the "Royal" sign of the Zodiac. If permitted full play by the other forces (those of heredity, environment, and education) it bestows such wonderful gifts and royal favors that it is one of the most fortunate of the signs.

Leo rules over the entertainment world, and an

exceptional number of outstanding figures in music, literature, theatre, and screen are naturally among its subjects. You are unusually artistic and creative. With training, which you can absorb more quickly than most people, you can generally find your place in one of these fields.

Your nature is kind and sympathetic; you are genial and good-hearted, with a tendency to make friends quickly. The social side of your life will always play a great part in your affairs, both romantic and commercial; you will prosper through your contact with important figures.

Leo is symbolized by the Lion. This suggests a predatory instinct, and you have it, though usually in a socialized and civilized form. You are aggressive, with unusual courage to combat life; when you set your whole mind on a certain goal, nothing short of death will stop you. Not quite ruthless, you nevertheless are inclined to worship power and money, to such an extent that you frequently force yourself to "like" a person because he can help you in reaching your goal. Your nature is high-spirited and adventurous. You like to roam about from place to place, and are apt to travel to far and strange places in your quest for adventure and excitement. Frankly, your predatory and ruthless tendencies are not likely to get out of hand, but if your personal heredity adds to their force, keep on your guard.

YOUR TRUE CHARACTER

Your chances for success, as I have indicated, are well above average in all departments of your life. This success may come quite early in your career. Moreover, you should have three separate chances to try for your goal, three cycles during which you can try again for fame and success if your previous attempts have failed. Such failure is most apt to come about from your inclination to be unwisely generous, to throw your money away carelessly, and to make poor investments. Your pocketbook is often easy prey for unscrupulous persons. You must guard these weaknesses with extra care, for your type is not inclined to learn by experience.

Emotionally, you are well balanced. Sentimental, sympathetic, and demonstrative, you will do anything for those you love. Your constant desire is for romantic happiness, and you are miserable and unhappy when out of love. Unfortunately, most Leo persons tend to make the wrong choice in love and generally suffer great unhappiness in one or more romances. They often marry twice. When you do make the right choice, however, you enjoy your home; you are fond of children, and if typical of your sign, should be blessed with two.

An examination of the lives of these famous persons, also born under the influences of Leo, may guide you in your problems: Statesmen Herbert

Hoover, Queen Elizabeth, Benito Mussolini; Authors George Bernard Shaw, Booth Tarkington, Edna Ferber, Gen. Hugh Johnson; men of business Henry Ford, Bernard Baruch; Actors Robert Taylor, Norma Shearer, William Powell, and Myrna Loy.

VIRGO

(Aug. 23–Sept. 22)

At the time of your birth the Sun was in the earth sign of Virgo. However, your ruling planet Mercury governs the mind and nerves. Consequently you are a strange combination of the earthy practical and mercurial mystic; of the commercial and artistic.

Your dominant characteristic is intensity. Your mind is rapid and restless, constantly probing the secrets of life and death; you are highly nervous and energetic. You burn up so much energy that you *must* have more rest than most people. Watch your diet, and exercise unusual precautions about your general health to escape the consequences of nervous reactions due to your amazing mental activity.

You must understand the pitfalls which your nature places in the paths of friendship and your human relations. You not only question the purpose of everything you yourself do, but constantly probe the motives of others. You are inclined to be somewhat suspicious of new people, "freezing" your personality into a formal and forbidding exterior, although once a person manages to penetrate this frigid wall he finds you charming, sociable and interesting. If you do a kind deed you prefer to keep it a secret; you seldom discuss your thoughts or actions with others. You value your privacy sometimes too highly, and resent fiercely any attempt to pry, snoop or meddle with your affairs.

As a matter of fact, some of your suspicion and tendency to thrust people away is justified. You have a tendency to involve yourself with people in ways harmful to your best interests; you should never sign legal papers or contracts without an unusually searching investigation. Oddly enough, you tend to thrust away the wrong persons; you have a tendency to become involved with relatives who will try to dominate your life, and must be especially cautious lest persons closest to you attempt to gain control of your interests and put you in subjugation.

Your chances for success in life are very strong. Virgo is one of the most intelligent and practical signs in the Zodiac. You have great ability in meeting people (when you break through your natural reserve) and are adaptable enough to fit into any environment. You are shrewd in business dealings, logical, discriminative, and methodical, and can be trusted with detail in business. You may well rise to a position of power through secret alliances or through persons in political positions.

Mercury gave you a sharp, analytical brain, adapted especially to scientific study and a searching insight into people and things. But your intensity and the rapidity of your mind leads to pitfalls. You are inclined to over-emphasize details and to demand unerring accuracy in your subordinates. Though quick to commend a good worker, you are just as quick to criticize and condemn one who is inept, slovenly, careless, or stupid. Provided you have learned patience and the art of making your criticism tactful and constructive, you make an excellent executive—competent, honest and efficient in your duties.

Emotionally, you are loyal and sincere, though inclined to be stand-offish and undemonstrative in your affections. Refined and sensitive, you have a love of poetry, art, literature and music. Your idealism, unusually high, is apt to lead you to more than one disappointment in early romance. I should warn you that your type is generally inclined to entangling alliances in romance which can cause mental unrest and unhappiness. You must constantly guard against unconventional situations and adverse publicity, avoiding even the appearance of guilt.

A study of the lives of the following famous persons, also born in your sign, should be helpful to you: Statesmen President William H. Taft, Queen Wilhelmina; Authors Leo Tolstoi, Oliver Wendell Holmes, Bret Harte, O. Henry, Upton Sinclair, H. G. Wells; advocate of birth control Margaret Sanger; Marquis de LaFayette and Cardinal Richelieu; Actors Fredric March, Greta Garbo, Joan Blondell, Fred MacMurray, Jackie Cooper, Claudette Colbert.

LIBRA

(Sept. 23–Oct. 22)

You were born in the air sign of Libra, and have the peaceful, beautiful planet Venus as your ruling star.

Your nature is kind and generous, one which loves above all else peace and quiet; abhorring quarrelling, confusion and discord. You take great pride in making a comfortable home, and in having everything about you trim and in perfect order. In fact, your resentment of untidiness and confusion is so marked that you should, as far as possible, surround yourself with people who respect your strong wishes in such matters. You will suffer from that very discord you abhor, or at least from inner unhappiness, unless you can cultivate tolerance and a realization that these things which seem so big to you may honestly be regarded as trivial by someone else.

Your mind is highstrung and intuitive, subject to strong impressions which are often fearful and lead to worry. You are inclined to hold back when you should push forward, and you find yourself constantly weighing one course against another to see which you should follow. This weighing is *not* indecision, but a wise deliberation and a tendency you should indulge. The symbol of your sign is the Scales, for the Ancients observed that persons born under this set of planetary influences constantly balance everything in life, seeing and considering both sides of every question. You are good at judging the right and wrong, and good and bad, and you should take the time you instinctively want in making decisions. Libra subjects seldom choose the wrong course, simply because of this fine sense of discrimination which they possess.

You probably worry about your inclination to sarcasm and fault-finding. It is a fact that persons dealing with you find you stubborn and strong-willed, but this tendency should not be entirely stamped out until you are absolutely sure of the person with whom you are dealing. This is a protective wall which Libra has erected around you, guarding you against the hazards to which your exceptionally easy-going, peace-loving nature would otherwise find you subject. In spite of this tendency to a sharp tongue, you are inclined to attract many friends; and they find you witty, amusing, and a good conversationalist. Your ability to use words gives you great influence over other persons, an influence which you must be careful to use in ways helpful to them.

You will never attain your ambitions. True, you will reach goal after goal, but upon reaching each one you will immediately set up another goal further ahead, never quite satisfied with what you have accomplished. Your obstacle is going to be a tendency to let your mind dwell on the negative things, often to such an extent that you may decide to simply stop trying, and sit back. This can be fatal, for, very frankly, Libra is a sign that requires a great deal of effort to attain recognition from the world. You have unusual characteristics, but you must exert more effort than most to capitalize on them.

You are not interested in fame and success for their own sakes alone, but you do like luxurious living and extravagant things. Therefore, money will always mean a great deal to you, because of the things you can get with it. And as I said before, you will never be quite satisfied with what you attain.

You are strongly attracted to creative work, and though you may be successful in executive work, you are best suited to working behind the scenes, where you can use your creative powers in an atmosphere of unhurried calm.

Study the lives of these famous persons, also born in your sign, to see how they capitalized their talents and overcame their handicaps: Statesmen John Marshall and William Penn; Presidents Chester Alan Arthur, Zachary Taylor, and Rutherford B. Hayes; thought-leaders Annie Besant and Nietzsche; Admiral Lord Nelson, Franz Liszt, Max Schmeling, Eleanor Roosevelt; Actresses Eleanor Duse, Greer Garson, Sarah Bernhardt, Constance Bennett, Janet Gaynor, Carole Lombard, Miriam Hopkins and Helen Hayes.

SCORPIO

(Oct. 23–Nov. 22)

At the time of your birth the Sun was in the water sign of Scorpio, and your ruling planet was Mars.

You were fortunate to be born in this strong, intuitive, and mystical sign, for good luck generally follows most Scorpio subjects throughout life.

Your sign gives you a love of the mystic and occult; you are gifted for study along Astrological and occult lines, though the outward evidence of this power is frequently an aptitude for the study and analysis of people. Many times this flair for penetration of character gives you ability as a writer or dramatic actor.

Scorpio persons usually possess a solid, heavy

figure (subject to heredity); they are blessed with good looks and dynamic personality. Their mysticism is betrayed by magnetic eyes which carry at times an almost hypnotic power. The voice is generally soft, pleasant, and refined; some of the greatest singers of history were born in this sign.

Your danger lies in your temper. Mars, the planet of war, is your ruler, and gives you a nature that is difficult at times for others to understand and get along with. You are apt to be volatile and explosive, dominating, and set on having your way. You are given to sudden biting outbursts of temper which terrify the unfortunate persons about you: but the storm subsides as fast as it arose and you can quickly be pacified by someone close to you, at which time you become as genial and pleasant as though nothing had ever happened. This tendency to blazes of temper and flaring moods must be controlled.

Your volatility leads to another weakness. You are prone to embark on some project with a burst of tremendous energy, only to give it up before you have carried it through to completion. Your ideas are generally sound, and should be carried through. You must learn to concentrate your energies and coördinate your life, lest all your efforts be fruitless through scattering.

The luck in your sign blesses you with excellent chances of success, provided you can overcome the handicaps I have mentioned and concentrate your energy into productive channels. Your mind is strong, your memory is good, and you have the knack of adaptability. Though you dislike physical labor, you have the power (if you will use it) of concentration, and can carry through any project you undertake, especially if you are overseeing it rather than doing the actual labor and detail work. You have a good mind for ideas, for the handling of money, and promoting the welfare of others.

A study of the lives of these famous persons, also born with your birthright of luck and volatility, will help you to understand yourself and your problems: Statesmen King Edward VII, Presidents James Abram Garfield, James Knox Polk and Theodore Roosevelt; Authors Robert Louis Stevenson, Macaulay; Cheiro, famous Astrologer; Martin Luther, Hetty Green, Samuel Insull, Father Charles Coughlin, Madame Eva Curie and Ignace Paderewski; Actors Will Rogers, Marie Dressler, Jackie Coogan, Hedy Lamarr, John Boles, Eleanor Powell, Dick Powell, and Vivien Leigh.

YOUR TRUE CHARACTER

SAGITTARIUS

(Nov. 23–Dec. 21)

Sagittarius is a fire sign, ruled by the planet Jupiter. You were born to rule, to govern and direct. You are not the type to submit willingly to the domination of others in business, romance, or the home. Friction often arises in your life because others do not understand this quality in your nature, or because they themselves have similar powers of domination which clash with yours.

Your success is apt, however, to be clouded by unhappiness. You are inclined to be moody and easily discouraged by adversity, sinking into long periods of despondency when things do not turn out as you wish them. You are sensitive, easily hurt by others, and a target for the unsympathetic barbs of those who misunderstand your motives. All these tendencies must be brought under control, your discouragements forgotten in a fresh onslaught, and your sensitiveness overlaid by a protective veneer.

Your nature in friendship is intense, loyal, affectionate and ardent. Not overly demonstrative, you have a tendency to surround yourself with a wall of aloofness which others cannot penetrate. However, to those you love and permit inside this wall you are indulgent and generous, permitting them many liberties which would be unthinkable to outsiders. Emotionally, you tend to be jealous. Since the full emotional force of the planets was directed on you at birth, your maturity is apt to be early. This maturity is apt to come to you before your reasoning judgment has developed to a corresponding degree, and you must exercise extra caution in your early romantic life to avoid mistakes which will bring unhappiness in their train.

Your influences at birth were commercial. You are logical, methodical, and painstaking in everything you do. Your best chance of success is in the business and financial world, where your accuracy and quickness of decision has full play. (I do suggest, however, that you develop your Sagittarian talent for music at least as a hobby. It is interesting to note that Sagittarians Deanna Durbin, Dorothy Lamour and Grace Moore were all born within five days of the same birthday.)

But try early to get into a position where you rule; in your own business, as a free agent, or in a free and responsible executive position. For you will not work well under the orders of others. Your greatest chance for a fortune comes in middle life, through investments in stocks and bonds, through real estate, or as a result of a legacy. It may reassure you to know that Jupiter brings you several chances in your lifetime to make your fortune.

YOUR TRUE CHARACTER

A study of the lives of these famous persons, also born under your sign, may give you guidance: Statesmen King George VI of England, Queen Alexandria, the Duke of Kent, Benjamin Disraeli, President Martin van Buren; Authors Mark Twain, John Greenleaf Whittier, John Milton, Noel Coward, Arthur Brisbane; Composer Ludwig van Beethoven; Philanthropist Andrew Carnegie; Actors Douglas Fairbanks Jr., Frances Dee, Edward G. Robinson, Marion Talley, and Dorothy Lamour.

CAPRICORN

(Dec. 22–Jan. 19)

Born while the Sun was in the earth sign of Capricorn, your ruling planet is Saturn.

You inherited a splendid brain from your birth sign. Though deliberate rather than rapid, you are capable of deep, sustained thought, and have great intellectual capacity. This mind of yours is orderly, systematic, and dignified. It gives to your bearing a regal air, an impression of solidity and dependability which makes you more distinguished than the subjects of most signs of the Zodiac.

You weigh carefully every word before you speak, and your opinion, when it comes, is generally very well worthwhile. You were born to lead rather than follow, a quality which other people usually feel instinctively and accept without question. When you have deep convictions about any matter, you should follow them through to the end.

Because your nature is hard to understand, you may make few real friends in life. Admirers of your qualities, yes, but not true friends: though those friends you do make will be loyal and sincere, sometimes to an almost fanatical degree. When problems arise which seem unsolvable, you should consult these friends. Your nature is one which must constantly strive to avoid depression and despair.

The symbol of Capricorn is the Goat. Like this obstinate animal, you are sometimes given to butting your head against stone walls. You are headstrong, determined, sometimes unreasonable. Perhaps your greatest fault is that of forcing your opinions on others, forgetting that they have a right to their own. You must guard against the waste of effort in trying to change the unchangeable and move the immovable.

You have, as I have indicated, unusual qualities of leadership. You can manage other people, or conduct a business of your own (avoiding, however, occupations which require snap judgment and lightning thought), and you should work constantly toward financial independence.

It is my distasteful obligation to warn you that the planet Saturn often brings trouble, obstacles and delays to your plans. It sometimes inclines to grave disturbances early in life, especially in connection with parents, sometimes producing lingering illness to you or your relatives. It is especially necessary for you to keep a guard over your health, and to be exceptionally cautious of accidents. You are also apt to burden yourself with unnecessary obligations on the part of relatives, and your pocketbook must be closely guarded to keep out the hands of the undeserving.

In your particular case, a study of famous companions in your sign of Capricorn will be most helpful: Statesmen Benjamin Franklin, Joseph Stalin, John Hancock, Daniel Webster, Alexander Hamilton, William Ewart Gladstone, Presidents Andrew Johnson and Woodrow Wilson; Authors Rudyard Kipling, Sir Isaac Newton, Louis Bromfield, Jack London, Alexander Woollcott; Actors Lew Ayres, Marlene Dietrich, Kay Francis, Anita Louise, Ray Milland.

AQUARIUS

(Jan. 20–Feb. 18)

At the time of your birth the Sun was in the air sign of Aquarius, and the planet Uranus was ruling the heavens.

Astrologers consider this to be one of the best

signs under which to be born. As a matter of fact, it is said that there are more Aquarius subjects in the Hall of Fame than any other sign. You were given a brilliant mind, with unusually active inventive and creative ability.

You have a very intuitive nature, which seldom plays you false and which endows you with an amazing understanding of life and people. Flowing from this is a fondness for mysticism, and a liking to work in secret ways. Listen to this star-given inner voice of yours; let it guide you in choosing your friends and designing your life work, and you are apt to find your plans maturing and fortune seeking you out.

Truly, your gifts are great. But nature has a way of balancing her gifts, and you have also two great handicaps. The first you can do nothing about: that is the expectation of encountering a great many obstacles in your progress. The second you can control: that is your strong tendency to dream rather than do.

Your sign is passive, and unless you force yourself into action, many splendid opportunities are going to slip through your fingers. This passivity leads to an inclination to rest on your laurels. Remember always that if you are to surmount the obstacles which will appear in your path you must expend unnatural effort, compelling yourself to be alert and progressive, fighting your natural tendency to sit back and wait for the world to recognize your unquestionably great talents.

These handicaps can be overcome. Edison's life was a constant struggle to overcome obstacles, chief among which, of course, was his deafness (I might mention in passing that Edison's gifts to modern civilization are typical of this sign, for Aquarius is symbolized by the Waterbearer: Aquarians tend constantly to be giving out to others, nourishing, sponsoring, developing those who come to them for guidance). Franklin Roosevelt is another Aquarian who overcame a natural obstacle.

Many times fame comes more easily to Aquarians who happen to develop their talents and set their goals early in life. Charles Lindbergh's phenomenal accomplishments are typical of the amazing careers often vouchsafed to those fortified by these vibrations.

In friendship, you are prone to be somewhat intolerant and impatient with persons of lesser gifts than yours. You must fight off this tendency, also your inclination to become aloof and unapproachable after you have attained distinction.

But most important of all, remember your peculiar necessity of keeping your feet on the ground and in motion toward your goal. Seek to maintain a balance between the practical and idealistic sides of your nature. Engage yourself in some practical, useful work where your great mental gifts can have full play; then either save your day-dreaming for out of hours, or convert it into imaginative, but practical and constructive, planning.

Study the lives of these famous companions of yours under the sign of Aquarius. They tended to have the same mental gifts, shackled by the same obstacles and passivity, as you. Statesmen Abraham Lincoln, Wm. McKinley, Aaron Burr, Franklin D. Roosevelt; Authors Lord Byron, Robert Burns, Charles Lamb, Jules Verne, Charles Dickens; Spiritual leaders Swedenborg, Dwight L. Moody; Scientists Thomas A. Edison, Charles Darwin, Galileo; Composer Wolfgang Mozart and Singer Adelina Patti; Actors Sir Henry Irving, John Barrymore, Ida Lupino, Ronald Colman, Adolph Menjou, Clark Gable, and Edgar Bergen.

PISCES

(*Feb. 19–Mar. 20*)

You were born in the water sign of Pisces, your ruling planet Neptune.

The symbol of Pisces is the Fishes. It is significant to note that one is swimming upstream, the other down. So it is with your life, in which a long period of failure may be broken with success—and vice versa, in that a smooth stretch of success may be interrupted by reverses, your life changing its direction. Fortunately, like the fish which fights its way through boiling rapids to its spawning place, you are gifted with unusual courage, determination, and tenacity. You generally overcome, with the aid of these qualities, the obstacles with which you are faced. If heredity or environment has robbed you of these natural qualities set about building them up, for you have within you unusual gifts and the power to capitalize them.

Neptune is the planet of beauty and mystery. It rules the shadowy and mysterious things of life, the secret life forces, and inclines you to spirituality and an interest in the occult and psychic. You will find yourself enjoying, and gifted for, the study of religion, philosophy, and the metaphysical.

Neptune also endowed you with vibrations approaching eternal youth: even at an advanced age, others will deem you much younger than you actually are. You should develop your latent talents, especially the leaning to music which most Pisces subjects have: you will find music exceptionally soothing in times of fatigue and stress.

You are happiest in a settled home of your own, and you should try to locate in the country if possible. Your fondness for the outdoors should be indulged, for you need exercise to keep in good health perhaps more than persons of other signs.

You have considerable personal magnetism, which attracts people and makes them your friends. Guard, however, against a tendency to be unapproachable, for your friends will misunderstand your motives. A greater hazard is your unusual sensitiveness. This rises in part from your affectionate and sentimental nature—it means more than it should to you to have your anniversaries remembered, and to receive little evidences of affection. You are too easily hurt by small slights, a tendency which in some Pisces persons gets out of hand and leads to the habit of imagining slights where none were intended. Try to overcome this inclination toward supersensitiveness.

Financial success means a great deal to you, for you have an unusually intense fear of old age and dependence on others. Fortunately, though your makeup is refined and intellectual, you are peculiarly adapted to commercial pursuits, with an instinctive understanding of business principles which others must work out for themselves. The best business for you is one which capitalizes your ability to meet the public and to handle other people. You are inclined to be fortunate in investments, especially as they concern your own business ventures and real estate, and you are the type who should set aside money for the purpose of entering business for yourself.

YOUR TRUE CHARACTER

Romance and marriage mean much to Pisces subjects. There are, however, unusual hazards for you: you are subject to mistakes in the choice of a mate which can cause you great grief. This particular aspect of the Pisces destiny is so complex that I prefer to defer a detailed discussion to the later chapter which deals with the subject at length.

Study the lives of these famous persons, also born under the sign of Pisces. You will find lessons in their lives which will be helpful in solving your own problems. Statesmen George Washington, James Madison, William Jennings Bryan, Andrew Jackson; Authors Voltaire, James Russell Lowell, Victor Hugo, Henry Wadsworth Longfellow, Elizabeth Barrett Browning; Composer Chopin; Actors Ellen Terry, Lillie Langtry, Madeline Carroll, Louis Hayward, Joan Bennett and John Garfield.

★ 3 ★

HOW TO SEEK ROMANTIC HAPPINESS

THE Sun has stamped each one of us with an indelible pattern of character. That character, that temperament and disposition, either harmonizes with the other Signs or clashes with them.

Let's suppose that you are Gemini, a dominating type. Would you naturally get along smoothly with the stubbornness of Aries? Of course not; but the passive Pisces would welcome your domination.

Just as certain chemicals explode when mixed, so do certain star-given temperaments, when combined in the intimacy of love, produce a reaction of brain and body which leads to emotional explosions. Other temperaments merge perfectly. It is my purpose here to analyze the romantic temperament of each Sign. Moreover, while each Sign considered by itself will react in a certain way, its reactions may be quite different in combination with each of the other Signs, so I must therefore explain which Signs are compatible and which incompatible when placed in relationship with each other.

Of course, in spite of anything anyone might say

you will keep right on falling in love with your opposites. I find no fault with that, for the stars do not dictate that you *must* clash with another person: they simply say that you *tend* to clash. If you *know* about those hidden characteristics of the other person which are apt to clash with yours, you can make allowances, handle him tactfully, and get along with that person almost as well as though the two of you had been born in perfect accord.

You can certainly remember some occasion on which you were very much annoyed by someone's irritability. But later you found that his irritability was caused by worry about the illness of a loved one, by business troubles, or something else which gave him good reason. And then you promptly forgave the hurt. You forgave it *because you now understood what caused that person to act as he did.*

I want you to learn patience, tolerance, and forbearance. If you do not get along with someone (and this chapter, I should mention, has a very real bearing on business contracts and friendships, as well as love), use the following pages to probe into his hidden character. Try to find what there is in his hidden nature, what inner compulsion causes him to do the things which clash with you. That fresh light of understanding will bring into your life a new harmony which you might have thought impossible.

I cannot over-emphasize the importance of this. Many a divorce could have been avoided if the husband and wife had only searched each other's characters and discovered the true cause (often tragically slight) of their disagreement. Many a tragic downfall could have been escaped had the headlong, impulsive person searched himself and realized what potent forces he should have fought. Many a person could have been saved from suicide had the people around him but realized what hidden desires in his nature made intolerable the atmosphere which they had unthinkingly created. Astrology gives the key to the hidden character, reveals the secret barriers which exist in the minds of those with whom we deal—and, above all, teaches patience, tolerance and forbearance with the secret forces which it has laid bare.

So when I say that a certain Sign is incompatible with yours, I am not erecting a "No Passing" sign in your road. Not even a "Detour." Rather, it reads "Caution." Watch for the pitfalls in the rough road more carefully than you would skim along the open highway of the compatible Sign.

In this chapter, read your own Sign to learn your own tendencies in romance and personal dealings. Find what negative characteristics you should control. Then read the Sign of the person in whom you are romantically interested.

HOW TO SEEK ROMANTIC HAPPINESS

A comparison of the two natures will throw a great deal of light on your problems. Under your Sign you will find a list of other Signs which are especially compatible or incompatible to yours, but a careful study of the sections themselves is vital if you are to know the reasons for these probable reactions.

We are interested here in personal contacts and romance in the broad sense. The next chapter, "How to Attract and Please the One You Love," is more specific, though both are concerned with attraction and romance in the conditions existing before marriage. The later chapter on "New Joy in Marriage" analyzes the different qualities which are brought out in the intimacy and day-to-day contact of the marital state.

But the theme which runs through all these chapters is the same—learn why the other person acts as he does. Then with that new understanding, cultivate a tolerance which will enrich your life with romantic satisfaction, and the serenity of perfect peace and harmony.

ARIES

(Mar. 22–Apr. 20)

Ruled by the fiery Mars, you have a tendency to outbursts of temper which result in hurts and misunderstandings. You are hasty in your judgments of others, and often you judge harshly. You often doubt unjustly the love of one who is by nature simply aloof and undemonstrative. Your inclination to hasty judgment makes it exceptionally necessary that you always search your heart closely to be certain you are taking the right steps in love.

You are very dominating. You like to impose your views, friends, likes and dislikes, and in fact your whole life pattern on the one you love, moulding him or her to your own taste. Partnership in romance with another dominating person, or with someone who does not understand and tolerate this trait in you, will lead to trouble.

Your strong possessiveness implies jealousy. You even resent the friends, acquaintances and outside interests of your loved one. You demand "all" of a person.

When you love, however, you are ardent and loyal. You expect and require absolute fidelity. Since you enjoy sharing your possessions and entertaining in a home of your own, marriage is the ideal state for you. Being so affectionate and sentimental, it is very important that you have a demonstrative and affectionate person in your life; if possible, one of the type which actually welcomes your domination and possessiveness.

You are generally happiest when in love, miserable

HOW TO SEEK ROMANTIC HAPPINESS

when you quarrel with your sweetheart. You should try very hard indeed to avoid such disturbances, for their upsetting effect on your mind and body causes you to be moody and depressed.

To Aries

COMPATIBLE SIGNS	INCOMPATIBLE SIGNS
Leo (*stimulating*)	Gemini (*dominating*)
Sagittarius (*intellectual*)	Scorpio (*jealous*)
Taurus (*practical*)	Cancer (*moody*)
Aquarius (*idealistic*)	Pisces (*too negative*)

(The Signs not mentioned have a neutral reaction: neither compatible nor incompatible. The reaction will be determined mainly by the heredity, environment and education of both persons.)

TAURUS

(Apr. 21–May 20)

Much like Aries, except for less stubbornness, you must be the leader in romance. Though you harmonize best when the loved one subjugates himself to your wishes and whims, you are fairly reasonable and do not absolutely demand complete control of his life and thoughts.

However, you are apt to be jealous and suspicious, resenting the friends of your sweetheart. You do not easily accept these friends, and you keenly resent any tendency of the other person to flirtation. You have a marked possessiveness.

You are inclined to be somewhat unconventional in romance, often involved in two affairs of the heart at the same time, and with at least one bitter lesson to learn before you go on to happiness in marriage. In fact, two or three serious romances usually occur in the Taurus early life, and there is a tendency to marry before you are sufficiently old or experienced to know your own mind. Your leaning toward overly hasty action makes it necessary not to break off a romance until you have considered the whole matter carefully enough to make absolutely certain that the two of you cannot agree.

You attract by physical magnetism as well as mental charm. Though you don't go to either extreme of moral laxity or prudery, yet you are practical, realistic, and quite frank. You are impatient with personality problems; also with dependence and with what you consider falsely modest reticence. You need to cultivate more idealism in romance, more restraint in your expressions of sentiment. Moreover, your tendency to be cynical, sarcastic or blunt leads to the necessity of curbing your temper and restraining your aptness to fuss and fidget at small actions of which you disapprove.

HOW TO SEEK ROMANTIC HAPPINESS

To Taurus

COMPATIBLE SIGNS	INCOMPATIBLE SIGNS
Virgo (*imaginative*)	Scorpio (*suspicious*)
Capricorn (*aggressive*)	Leo (*dominating*)
Cancer (*intuitive*)	Sagittarius (*possessive*)
Pisces (*passive*)	Aquarius (*dependent*)

(The Signs not mentioned have a neutral reaction: neither compatible nor incompatible. The reaction will be determined mainly by the heredity, environment and education of both persons.)

GEMINI

(May 21–June 20)

In the early stages of acquaintanceship, and sometimes even later, you give an impression of being aloof and cold. You should make an especial effort to be more approachable in romance and friendship.

The typical Gemini is attracted more by intellectual things than physical. You enjoy the companionship of the person you love, like to discuss your mutual interests, share your joys and sorrows. It is only after a long or close association that you become intimate, especially in the physical sense. You cannot love for long a person who has nothing but physical magnetism to offer.

YOU AND THE STARS

You enjoy the companionship of the opposite sex, and you attract its members quickly. But you are not so capable in holding their love, since you tire quickly and turn to someone new. The duality in your nature may bring great unhappiness to you, as well as to the person who is hurt by your fickleness and flirtatiousness. You must learn to merge the dual parts of your nature into one, cultivating constancy, sincerity, and fidelity, these desirable qualities usually being foreign to your nature. You must also guard against being too dominating or possessive, for you share with Aries and Taurus the tendency to be jealous, caustic, and quick to outbursts of temper.

You will have more than one love affair early in life. Depending upon how soon you bring your duality under control, you may have as many as five or six really serious romances before settling down to the one person who you feel can make you happy.

To Gemini

COMPATIBLE SIGNS	INCOMPATIBLE SIGNS
Libra (*creative*)	Aries (*stubborn*)
Aquarius (*emotional*)	Leo (*critical*)
Gemini (*sensitive*)	Sagittarius (*moody*)
Pisces (*mystical*)	Capricorn (*reticent*)

(The Signs not mentioned have a neutral reaction: neither compatible nor incompatible. The reaction will be determined mainly by the heredity, environment, and education of both persons.)

CANCER

(June 21–July 22)

Your Sign, ruled by the Moon, makes you emotional, intense, idealistic, and given to daydreaming.

You have a tendency to build up an idealized image of the one you love, often setting a standard so high that no ordinary human being can measure up to it. You are correspondingly hurt and disillusioned when you discover ordinary human weaknesses in the one you love, especially when such weaknesses offend your moral, sensitive and conventional nature. You resent crudity, and retreat from a nature which is too aggressive: you must be wooed with tenderness and gentleness. I must warn you that cruel disappointments lie ahead unless you force yourself to be more realistic, less exacting and less critical, willing to make some of the necessary adjustments and sacrifices yourself. The harmonizing of any two personalities is a process of give and take; it is going to be hard for you to "give."

You are generally fortunate in attracting members of the opposite sex, due largely to your appealing modesty, winning smile, and your sympathetic understanding of other people's problems. You are by nature most agreeable and genial to the one you love, and although you have some inclination to fickleness, you can easily cultivate constancy in romance. Constancy flows naturally from your in-born fastidiousness.

You must be careful lest two, or even more, persons fall in love with you at the same time: even more careful lest you be loved by someone who is already married. Should this happen, you more than almost any other Sign must take every precaution to keep from some action which you will bitterly regret later.

In general, you can afford to wait for the right choice, for you are not the type to be long defeated in romance: if you lose the one you love, you can forget quickly and turn to someone else.

There is ultimate happiness in romance for you. If disappointed, you should make every effort to take heart and try again, for life without romance is worthless to you.

To Cancer

COMPATIBLE SIGNS	INCOMPATIBLE SIGNS
Scorpio (*leader*)	Aries (*garrulous*)
Pisces (*coöperative*)	Leo (*fickle*)
Taurus (*aggressive*)	Sagittarius (*depressed*)
Virgo (*industrious*)	Gemini (*dual*)

62

HOW TO SEEK ROMANTIC HAPPINESS

(The Signs not mentioned have a neutral reaction to you: neither compatible nor incompatible. The reaction will be determined mainly by the heredity, environment and education of both persons.)

LEO

(July 23–Aug. 22)

Leo rules the heart and emotions.

You therefore love deeply and passionately. The loss of the one you love is almost a knockout blow. Even a lovers' quarrel leads you to brood and be despondent until the disagreement is overcome. The one who enters upon a love affair with you must realize this intensity of your romantic nature and be prepared to take matters as seriously as you do.

For your part, you must cultivate more calmness and poise in your love life. Moreover, you must guard your inclination to be critical and sarcastic when misunderstandings arise, and to be impatient with mistakes by the one you love. You tend to be overly hasty in forming your decisions and in condemning others.

You are difficult to win, for you are very popular with members of the opposite sex, always with a little group of admirers about you. Your sweetheart must be of the type which is not prone to jealousy, or at least one who has such a tendency under control.

You are most apt to attract persons who are in the professions, the arts, or finance.

Usually you meet those who prove to be romantically interested in you through the normal channels, for your Sign is predominantly formal and conventional. Buried in your character, however, is the power to go to the opposite extreme of laxity and unconventionality, against which you must constantly guard.

To Leo

COMPATIBLE SIGNS	INCOMPATIBLE SIGNS
Aries (*emotional*)	Gemini (*critical*)
Sagittarius (*sensitive*)	Cancer (*fickle*)
Leo (*artistic*)	Pisces (*restless*)
Aquarius (*sympathetic*)	Scorpio (*sarcastic*)

(The Signs not mentioned above have a neutral reaction to you: neither compatible nor incompatible. The reaction will be determined mainly by the heredity, environment and education of both persons.)

VIRGO

(Aug. 23–Sept. 22)

You are inclined to choose romantic partners with about the same educational and social background as your own. This is well, because you live more on the intellectual plane than the physical, and do not enjoy for long the companionship of any person, even in romance, unless you have mental interests in common. These may include occupational interests, as well as the arts and hobbies. You must be able to like and respect a person before you can love him.

Your natural reserve leads new acquaintances to consider you cold and unemotional, though actually you can be intense and passionate. When you fall in love you give yourself wholeheartedly and without reservation. Nevertheless, you are basically the companion type rather than an emotional sweetheart, and your confidence and liking must be won over a long period of time before you can let down the barriers you have erected around your heart. You are slightly ashamed of emotion, in fact, and try to suppress any outward evidences of deep feeling.

Once in love, you are loyal, and willing to sacrifice your own comforts and preferences to make your beloved happy. You even permit mental abuse and subjugate yourself to the loved one, though this rises somewhat from your intense dislike of discord and upset. Often you carry this submission too far, sacrificing your career, friends, even relatives to the selfish desires of one who loves you.

It is unusually important, therefore, that you search your heart closely in romance to make certain you are giving your heart to a person worthy of it, one who will not abuse your gift. Though you flatter yourself that you choose more on a basis of reason than emotion or infatuation, nevertheless you can be won by a sympathetic person who knows how to flatter you subtly, a person whose cleverly concealed true self may have ulterior motives, arousing your love only to cast it aside or abuse it later on.

You generally find happiness in love after a trial and error cycle. When you do decide on one person you are usually willing to wait for months or even years until obstacles are cleared away. You are easy to get along with in romance—too easy, as I indicated above, for your own good. You can be easily dominated by anyone who has won your confidence and love. You are apt to stick to a bad bargain rather than cause hurt or discord in breaking away.

To Virgo

COMPATIBLE SIGNS	INCOMPATIBLE SIGNS
Taurus (*conservative*)	Scorpio (*dominating*)
Cancer (*home loving*)	Aquarius (*secretive*)
Capricorn (*aggressive*)	Leo (*jealous*)
Pisces (*coöperative*)	Aries (*possessive*)
Virgo (*same interests*)	

(The Signs not mentioned above have a neutral reaction to you: neither definitely compatible nor incompatible. The reaction will be determined mainly by the heredity, environment and education of both persons.)

HOW TO SEEK ROMANTIC HAPPINESS

(Sept. 23–Oct. 22)

Ruled by the romantic planet Venus, you cherish the beauty in love more than its emotional and physical side.

If you choose correctly, you will fall in love with someone who is on a high intellectual plane, one who has social position and power, and generally one who is financially well-to-do. You will not consciously let the matter of money influence your choice, but it nevertheless is a strange fact that few Libra women fall in love with or marry men who do not have at least the prospect of rising to the top in their professions. You prefer the creative and artistic types to the commercial, and tend to be attracted to actors, singers, musicians, artists and writers.

Being somewhat impractical and visionary, you should try to attract someone who is more practical than you are, though I admit that such a choice is foreign to your inner preferences.

You are hard to please in love. Being naturally dominating, critical, and possessive, you often demand that the beloved make himself over to suit your preferences. Frequently this is difficult for him, since your mind is complex and hard to understand.

Among the less desirable Libra traits are those of

temper, cynicism and brusqueness. You are apt to be outspoken in romantic disputes and let these faults cause great harm. During courtship you are able to present a very beautiful side to your nature to anyone you love; but it is unfair and dangerous to shield him too much from the real "you."

You are happiest when instilling your personal philosophy and intellectual ideas into the mind of the one you love. You are generally fortunate, however, in attracting someone whom you can mould to suit your own nature and preferences.

To LIBRA

COMPATIBLE SIGNS	INCOMPATIBLE SIGNS
Gemini (*intellectual*)	Taurus (*sarcastic*)
Aquarius (*idealistic*)	Capricorn (*moody*)
Leo (*progressive*)	Scorpio (*cynical*)
Aries (*generous*)	Sagittarius (*suspicious*)
Virgo (*loyal*)	

(The Signs not mentioned above have a neutral reaction to you: neither definitely compatible nor incompatible. The reaction will be determined mainly by the heredity, environment, and education of both persons.)

SCORPIO

(Oct. 23–Nov. 22)

You are sexually very magnetic, with a decided physical appeal to members of the opposite sex.

HOW TO SEEK ROMANTIC HAPPINESS

There is a pitfall here, for, especially in romance with types such as Libra, you must guard against letting your strong sensuous impulses overbalance the mental and spiritual sides of your nature.

You must be the leader in romance, for you are set in your ways and apt to disagree violently with the opinions of the beloved. You are quite temperamental, jealous, suspicious and inclined to be brutally harsh in anger. You become sullen or pouty when crossed or opposed. Frankly, you can bring untold agony into the lives of those you love, for without constant watchfulness you develop a callousness of feeling. Generally speaking, you can restrain your feelings in romance, and there is even a tendency for you to become calculating; scheming to attract and exploit someone who can be of help in some project you are planning. This trait is found usually only in the lower nature of Scorpio, but it is there and you must guard against it.

It is vitally important that you find romantic happiness, for you are depressed, moody and miserable when not in love.

You are generally very loyal and inclined to do almost anything for your beloved: but ONLY if your love has been deeply stirred. When you feel that someone is really worthy of your great love, you can work, sacrifice, and struggle against overwhelming odds for his sake.

YOU AND THE STARS

To Scorpio

COMPATIBLE SIGNS	INCOMPATIBLE SIGNS
Cancer (*artistic*)	Aries (*quarrelsome*)
Pisces (*spiritual*)	Taurus (*dominating*)
Gemini (*intellectual*)	Leo (*egotistical*)
Sagittarius (*stimulating*)	Virgo (*aggressive*)
Capricorn (*humorous*)	Libra (*caustic*)

(The Signs not mentioned above have a neutral reaction to you: neither definitely compatible nor incompatible. The reaction will be determined mainly by the heredity, environment and education of both persons.)

SAGITTARIUS

(*Nov. 23–Dec. 21*)

You are apt to be rather depressed and moody. The best choice for you is someone whose bright, optimistic outlook cheers and encourages you when things seem to be going wrong.

Perhaps your greatest fault in romance is your tendency to burden your beloved with too many of your small personal problems, even to the point of whining.

You lean on the one you love, and that person can make or break your life. It is therefore vitally important that you seek a long time before making your final choice in romance.

You are seldom influenced by the other person's

money or position in life, for you love him for himself alone. Being unusually adaptable, you can choose your romantic partner from almost any stratum in life: you can find much in common with a person from the varied ranks of commerce, the professions, or the arts. Your attraction lies largely in your unusual qualities of loyalty and patience. You make few demands, though you can be hurt deeply by someone who flirts or tries deliberately to arouse your jealousy.

Your pitfall lies in depending too much upon one person in romance, with bitter hurt in store for you if the love affair ends unhappily. If such a thing should come to you, do not let it shatter your life: be warned in advance and set about readjusting your mind, forcing yourself to accept another romance. Your chances for finding happiness in love, however, are excellent, and you are generally inclined to early marriage.

To Sagittarius

COMPATIBLE SIGNS	INCOMPATIBLE SIGNS
Aries (*intellectual*)	Gemini (*sarcastic*)
Leo (*leadership*)	Cancer (*talkative*)
Scorpio (*creative*)	Libra (*caustic*)
Virgo (*home-loving*)	Taurus (*conceited*)
Sagittarius (*sympathetic*)	

YOU AND THE STARS

(The Signs not mentioned above have a neutral reaction to you: neither definitely compatible nor incompatible. The reaction will be determined mainly by the heredity, environment and education of both persons.)

CAPRICORN

(Dec. 22–Jan. 19)

More than anything else in life you need love and understanding. By nature you lead rather a lonely life which must be lightened by companionship. In love, you are stimulated, dynamic, progressive. Out of love, you are often depressed and moody.

But your ruler Saturn often causes romance to be delayed in your life, or puts obstacles in the way of its consummation. You must be extraordinarily careful not to attract or fall in love with someone who is already engaged or married.

Love comes to your heart only after knowing the other person for some time. You generally find this person in your everyday life: in business, or through some present friend. It is seldom a chance acquaintance, for your Sign is too conventional for that.

You are physically attractive to the opposite sex. Too, your ready smile, wit, and your genial spirit of good fellowship makes you easy to understand and get along with. You have few emotional problems, and are not very complex mentally.

You get along best with a rather sophisticated

type, and though you like a home environment, it does not mean as much to you as to some others. You are sociable and like going out.

Watch for trouble which may come through the interference of relatives. Watch also your own nature, for you can be very dominating on occasion, insisting upon your own way and refusing your sweetheart the privilege of having opinions of his own. Unfortunately you often attract a person who is inclined to flirt and seek the attentions of others, and you are too prone to combat this the wrong way —with stubbornness, unreasonableness, and rages which build up a small difference into a big issue.

Your nature requires that you cultivate sympathetic understanding and a willingness to make some sacrifices in love. Granted this, your chances for finding romantic happiness are very great, and if at first you are not successful, you should keep on trying until you find the person who is compatible in every way.

To Capricorn

COMPATIBLE SIGNS	INCOMPATIBLE SIGNS
Taurus (*affectionate*)	Gemini (*dual*)
Virgo (*industrious*)	Leo (*temperamental*)
Scorpio (*attractive*)	Libra (*social*)
Pisces (*magnetic*)	Aquarius (*negative*)
	Aries (*forceful*)

YOU AND THE STARS

(The Signs not mentioned above have a neutral reaction to you: neither definitely compatible nor incompatible. The reaction will be determined mainly by the heredity, environment, and education of both persons.)

(Jan. 20–Feb. 18)

Your Sign is the most idealistic in the entire Zodiac. You are in love with love, and romance can be something very beautiful and inspiring in your life.

But you go to extremes in romance. If you permit the negative side of your romantic nature to develop, love can overbalance your life, and you may even find your ruin in what should have been kept an ennobling and elevating emotion.

Seldom do you know your own mind and heart. You are extraordinarily popular with the opposite sex, but you are always falling in and out of love. Especially in your youth, you tend to make one mistake after another. Superficial people attract you; you fall in love with the magnetic personality, the brilliant conversationalist, the person of prominent position, only to find (perhaps too late) that their hidden qualities are undesirable.

Aquarius is an oft-married sign. Fight your natural tendency to let your heart rule your head, or expect the future to be full of heartbreak and confusion;

too high a price to pay for the pleasurable emotional excitement. John Barrymore, Clark Gable, Adolph Menjou are all Aquarians, and all much married.

To Aquarius

COMPATIBLE SIGNS	INCOMPATIBLE SIGNS
Gemini (*idealistic*)	Capricorn (*negative*)
Libra (*creative*)	Taurus (*dominating*)
Sagittarius (*emotional*)	Cancer (*moody*)
	Virgo (*aloof*)

(The Signs not mentioned above have a neutral reaction to you: neither definitely compatible nor incompatible. The reaction will be determined mainly by the heredity, environment, and education of both persons.)

PISCES

(Feb. 19–Mar. 20)

You are rather passive and negative in love. Easily led by others, you are the type to fall in love at first sight. Due to this easily influenced nature, you should not marry quickly after falling in love. Wait a few months to make sure of your real feelings.

In spite of your responsive nature, you are inclined to seem somewhat cold and aloof, not showing outwardly that you are in love. If you really want to attract and hold someone, you must break through this wall and let your affection be shown.

You enjoy companionship and the simple things

of life. You do not require constant entertainment, and although you appreciate the value of money, you seldom consider finances in choosing a sweetheart. Though you like an atmosphere of peace and quiet, your passive nature makes you easy to get along with.

The best mate for you is one who is positive in nature, but considerate, trusting and tactful. Jealousy or suspicion on his part will kill romance for you. You demand your own way so seldom that you are easily handled, but your unusual sensitiveness makes you easily hurt. Frankly, you must learn to curb this sensitivity, for it can cause you much unnecessary unhappiness. Your beloved will find that you are progressively minded, with a liking for developing yourself along his own mental lines.

If you have a positive quality, it is your liking for neatness and orderliness. You demand especially that the loved one be particular—perhaps much more particular than his nature permits—about matters of dress, home habits, and care of the body.

Your affections, despite the fact that they are quickly given, are everlasting. You are happiest with a beloved who is intelligent, musical or artistic, especially one who has some spiritual quality in his personality. Your chances for happiness in romance are very great.

HOW TO SEEK ROMANTIC HAPPINESS

To Pisces

COMPATIBLE SIGNS	INCOMPATIBLE SIGNS
Cancer (*emotional*)	Aries (*forceful*)
Scorpio (*balanced*)	Leo (*talkative*)
Taurus (*progressive*)	Sagittarius (*moody*)
Gemini (*capable*)	Libra (*dominating*)
Virgo (*practical*)	
Capricorn (*affectionate*)	

(The Signs not mentioned above have a neutral reaction to you: neither definitely compatible nor incompatible. The reaction will be determined mainly by the heredity, environment and education of both persons.)

★ 4 ★

HOW TO ATTRACT AND PLEASE
THE ONE YOU LOVE

LOVE at first sight! A sunlit morning, a passing look: a stormy evening, a cozy nook—two people meet, a spark is struck between them, and they stand on the threshold of romance.

It happens that way sometimes, but not as often as in books. In the real life of today you are much more apt to single out some person as desirable, then deliberately try to attract him or her to you. Later on, the spark is struck. But even then, the budding romance must be carefully nurtured and fostered until it develops into real love.

How is it to be done?

Well, think back to a time in your childhood when you desperately wanted your father to buy something for you. First, you made certain that your Mother had all his favorite dishes for dinner; then you were very careful indeed to do all the things you knew he approved of, and none of the things which you knew might displease him.

HOW TO ATTRACT THE ONE YOU LOVE

Human nature doesn't change much with the years. So when you find the person you want to attract romantically, and when the association has begun and you are thinking about making it strong and secure, just go back to that old formula. Make yourself into the sort of person your beloved prefers: do the things he likes, and avoid the things of which his nature leads him to disapprove.

In this chapter I will tell you the inner characteristics of each Sign which enter into romance and attraction. Incidentally, this knowledge is almost equally useful to you in matters of business and friendship: even more valuable when you are puzzled about the basic cause of disagreements and incompatibilities in courtship and marriage. Since the characteristics of men are different from those of women born in the same Sign, I will treat them separately.

So if it is a man you want to attract or please, learn here what he likes or dislikes, then act accordingly. If it is a woman who claims your heart, find here her secret inclinations in romance, and your chances of winning and holding her love will be just that much greater.

TO ATTRACT AND PLEASE AN ARIES WOMAN

The typical Aries woman, subject of course to the other natural influences of heredity, environment and education, leans more to the mental plane than the physical.

Appeal to her through her sense of reason rather than her emotions. She will like you to be cultured and refined, courteous and well read. She will expect you to share her cultural interests. As long as you respect her judgment and common sense you will find her reasonable, but make any attempt to boss her or force your opinions on her and she will become stubborn as the Ram which symbolizes Aries.

She enjoys the companionship of others, and resents being monopolized. You will be a step ahead if you have a circle of charming and intelligent friends for her to meet. She enjoys entertaining and being entertained, and though her tastes tend to extravagance, a frank discussion of your problems will find her wholeheartedly coöperative and understanding.

Your Aries woman likes to mother her man; she enjoys a feeling that you are dependent upon her. She will appreciate your going to her with your new ideas and projects, and you'll find yourself expanding and growing under the stimulation of her mental energies. You can depend upon her sympathy and helpful understanding in your personal problems. Though not overly sentimental, she likes affection and enjoys the little attentions and courtesies. Incidentally, even though it may be temporarily submerged by her heredity and bringing-up, she has a strong liking for outdoor sports and athletics.

Certain things are especially distasteful to your Aries woman.

Things to Avoid with Aries Women

Public criticism is fatal; in fact, she will resent criticisms or suggestions even when you are alone unless they are constructive and made with the acme of tact.

Unpunctuality especially annoys her: the fact that she is seldom on time herself is not an acceptable excuse.

Do not try to monopolize her time and attentions, for she needs some privacy and solitude out of each day.

Avoid sarcasm, "smartness," rude slang, and crudities.

Cater to her fastidiousness by being careful about the tidiness of your person and dress.

TO ATTRACT AND PLEASE AN ARIES MAN

A man born in this strong and positive Sign likes to dominate, to lead in all things of life, including romance. Permit him complete freedom in making plans and arrangements, and let him express his opinions freely.

He has a peculiar appeal, when you know him well: quite like a little boy who leans on his mother for protection. He likes the maternal in women, and enjoys having complete and perfect companionship with the woman of his choice. Rough as Aries Spencer Tracy may be in a screen role, you always sense that undercurrent of appeal to your maternal instincts.

Your Aries man is usually magnetic and charming, to others as well as you. He enjoys his harmless popularity and should be permitted his little flirtations. There will always be women about him, but once you have won his heart you will usually find him loyal, affectionate, and very sincere.

His interests are largely intellectual, but this leaning is not so pronounced as it is in the Aries woman. Still, though you can appeal to him with purely physical charm, the romance will not last long unless you back it up with intelligence and humour. He is, however, especially early in your association, easily swayed by beautiful music, exotic scents, soft lights, and attractive clothes.

Oddly enough, in spite of his domination he is rather modest when it comes to romance, and needs a good deal of subtle encouragement (remember I said "*subtle*"). Once you have attracted him he is comparatively easy to hold, for he is very loyal and intense. Be careful, however, to exhibit none of that possessiveness and jealousy which he will so actively resent.

HOW TO ATTRACT THE ONE YOU LOVE

THINGS TO AVOID WITH ARIES MEN

Do not be aggressive upon first meeting: if you are attracted to him, at least let him *think* he is doing the courting.

Avoid any appearance of meddling in his business affairs.

He has an intense dislike of affectation and pretension, so don't try to impress him with social position or importance. Be as natural and unaffected as you can.

TO ATTRACT AND HOLD A TAURUS WOMAN

The ruling Venus is the planet of beauty and gives to the Taurus woman, if heredity permits, great physical beauty and charm.

You will find her sentimental and affectionate, and very attractive to men. Probably the best way to her heart is by being attentive and affectionate. She relishes flattery even when she knows (or could know, if she would admit it) that its purpose is simply to appeal to her emotions. She likes gifts, and the more impractical they are, the better: perfumes, flowers, jewelry, and the like. But she values the sentiment more than the gift itself, and though her taste in dress and accessories is exacting, she does not demand that gifts be extravagant.

Your Taurus girl is highly idealistic and romantic. Modern though she may seem, deep down she would like to be wooed and won in the old-fashioned tradition, with all the swashbuckling gallantry of olden days.

She is easy to get along with, is a good conversationalist, and can hold her own equally well in social life, business, or the world of sports. If your first meeting occurs at a social function, you can best impress her by seeming intelligent, and somewhat retiring: if your first meeting is under business surroundings, an impression of being efficient, orderly and punctual will be best. She will measure you against her ideals, so guard against any betrayal of your weaknesses until you can count on her making allowances.

Good food mellows her mood. She likes to go to new places to eat, and she is in her element when trying out new dishes, either in a restaurant or in a kitchen at home.

THINGS TO AVOID WITH TAURUS WOMEN

Don't try to change her ways of thinking, for she feels she has a right to her private opinions.

Being quite set in her ways, you should not try to force her into going anywhere or seeing anyone against her wishes.

Do not quarrel or argue with her; she dislikes confusion and discord intensely.

Her liking for proper speech and writing makes it necessary for you to watch your grammar and choice of words.

Avoid the appearance of being mercenary, miserly or stingy, for her generous nature is opposed to those traits.

TO ATTRACT AND HOLD A TAURUS MAN

Your Taurus man is inclined to be earthy, and rather hearty. He likes the solid comforts, good food and drink, and enjoys to the full all manner of pleasures. He will like you to take your place with him in outdoor sports: he naturally prefers male companions on hunting trips and the like, but on other excursions your company is welcome.

He is apt to act more on emotion than on reason: an appeal to his sentimental nature is more effective than argument. You will get along with him best if you take him as he is and refrain from trying to change him too radically. He will probably not require much alteration, anyway, for he should be witty and charming: his ruling planet Venus makes him very sociable and friendly. But Taurus being a fixed Earth sign, he does not like to be jarred from his self-complacent rut. Remember that, and try instead to mould yourself to fit his character and background.

Taurus being practical, interested in business and money, you should be well up on business trends and financial matters if you discuss them with him: otherwise stay away from those topics or stick to safe generalities. He will enjoy political discussions and educational projects. Try to accept his hobbies for your own, if you would spend much time with him.

He admires beauty of face and figure. Lacking a fine sense of discrimination, bright colors appeal to him. Somber colors are good only when the costume has a sharp contrast. Though he has no detailed idea of what is smart, he instinctively likes the latest fashions. Don't consult him about changes in your clothing, hair-do, and other matters of appearance: he will think he dislikes change, but he actually relishes innovations. His fondness for naturalness makes it wise to use make-up sparingly and skillfully.

Even after you win his love you must fight to hold it. That liking for beauty gives him a roving eye, regardless of your attractiveness. If his interest in you wanes, try some innovation on your own part, or bring a fresh enthusiasm to your participation in something he especially enjoys doing.

THINGS TO AVOID WITH TAURUS MEN

Don't talk about other men and their good points, especially former sweethearts and husbands: avoid making him jealous.

Don't involve him with your relatives, and keep from imposing obligations on him or making appointments not to his taste.

Avoid unpunctuality; suppress any extravagant habits.

Don't go in for too much night-life, even though he seems to like it; he will tire of it easily.

TO ATTRACT AND PLEASE A GEMINI WOMAN

Your life with a Gemini woman may be exasperating, but it will never be dull.

Like the metal named for her ruling planet Mercury, she is elusive and you can never be quite sure of her. Just as you think you have your hand on her, she slips through your fingers.

Your approach must be cautious: she must see you many times before she cares for you, and even then the strange duality in her mind may make her uncertain in her choice between you and someone else. She likes intrigue, and anything can happen in your romance.

She may suddenly become angry and upset for no apparent reason: she may even choose to avoid you completely for a while; only to greet you later with a smile, ready to go on with the romance as though nothing had happened. This gives you a clue to some of the things you can expect from these fascinating Gemini women, but they make up for their mercurial temperaments by possessing more than their share of beauty, charm, and personality.

You will almost surely find her charming and cultured. Being attractive, witty, an interesting conversationalist, and a good sport, she is quite naturally popular with other men. When she knows you well and you have her complete trust, she will share the pleasures which you especially like, for she is pleasure-loving and has very high spirits. She does not respond any too well to details of your career and business, so avoid talking shop; talk instead about what is going on in the world and among your acquaintances.

Prepare for jealousy and suspicion, even though unjustified: do your best to avoid even an appearance of unfaithfulness. I warn you that she is highly intuitive and can feel whether you really love her alone or are sharing your love with someone else: she is hard to deceive. The duality in her nature makes her hard to understand and get along with. You must be extraordinarily careful to keep from hurting her tender feelings, for she is sensitive, high-strung, and inclined to nervousness. You must handle her diplomatically, and without harshness.

THINGS TO AVOID WITH GEMINI WOMEN

Repress any tendency you may have to be temperamental, impatient or quarrelsome. Keep away from controversial subjects.

Don't take your problems to her, for they are apt to depress her.

Don't try to regulate her life, habits, or friends: she is very independent by nature.

Avoid getting yourself involved with other persons: watch any carelessness in your habits of dress.

HOW TO ATTRACT THE ONE YOU LOVE

TO ATTRACT AND PLEASE A GEMINI MAN

A man born in this Sign is creative, artistic, imaginative and inventive. There is a wide field of interest here in which to capture and hold his attention.

But don't push yourself forward, for he is quite talkative and likes center stage. Be attentive: let him talk to his heart's content about his life and loves, his business and financial problems, his family and friends. He is usually involved with a circle of intimates, and you should give him full freedom to talk and reminisce about them no matter how much it may bore you.

So never try to monopolize a conversation with him. Whatever you do say, however, must be plain and frank, for he dislikes affectation of any kind. He demands complete honesty from you in word, thought, and deed.

He is conservative, and dislikes intensely any show of emotion in public: is by nature opposed to ostentation or demonstrative sentiment. Be a little reserved and reticent in romance with him. In fact, you will find him a bit cold emotionally, since he is more on the mental side than physical. He is fond of solitude: likes the country for rest and relaxation, but prefers to live in a city where he can mix with people when he wishes to. Don't try to drag him on a strenuous social round.

Your Gemini man will not be easy to win. But once you have earned his confidence and love, you will have a loyal and trustworthy sweetheart for life. His duality of temperament is not as trying as that of a Gemini woman, for he represses it: nevertheless, he is easily annoyed and is impatient with anyone who reacts slowly. Be prepared for rapid changes in his plans, for he makes lightning decisions and resents delay.

THINGS TO AVOID WITH GEMINI MEN

Don't intrude without invitation on his private life and thoughts.

Avoid offending his conservatism with any unconventionality in speech, dress or actions. He is quite apt to disapprove of your smoking or drinking.

Suppress any tendency to fits of temper, confusion, or discord.

Don't try to tell him what to eat and wear, or force your friends on him if he seems not to like them.

TO ATTRACT AND PLEASE A CANCER WOMAN

The keynote of the Cancer nature is its changeability.

If you are attracted to a Cancer woman you must work overtime to capture her interest and hold it.

She is very romantic and sentimental, and she can be devoted and loyal: but you never know when someone else is going to come along and attract her interest away from you.

She has social aspirations and enjoys people. She likes to be on the go constantly, and never seems to tire. Her restless nature demands constant activity, and if you can keep up with her you are well along the road to winning her approval.

This Sign is ruled by the changeable Moon, which makes her moody and sensitive. You must be understanding: patient with her shortcomings and careful about calling them to her attention. She responds with affection and looks for protection to a man who is capable, aggressive and even dominating. If you help her make up her mind when she is indecisive you'll save much wear and tear on your patience.

The typical Cancer woman is interested in the home and everything connected with it, whether arranging and furnishing it, cooking, or housekeeping details. She likes children, and generally is interested in child welfare or other social work.

You will probably appeal to her best if your nature is gentle and fastidious: and if your tastes run to the theatre, sports, travel, books, and music. Still, she admires progressive men, and is impressed with good financial prospects or one who has a high goal in social and business life and some chance of attaining it. Set up a high ideal and work toward it, if you would please her deeply.

Things to Avoid with Cancer Women

Don't be slovenly or careless in dress and manners.
Refrain from discussing your personal affairs in public.
Avoid extravagance, for she admires thrift.
Don't criticize her in the presence of others.

To Attract and Please a Cancer Man

Your typical Cancer man is just as changeable as the woman born under that Sign, but much easier to handle if you go about it properly.

His mind is centered more on business and financial success than social prestige or pleasures. He is easy to please, and does not demand constant entertainment.

You can attract him best by being his equal mentally. He likes beauty in women, but infinitely prefers someone who, though only moderately attractive physically, is intelligent, companionable, witty, and a vivid conversationalist. He enjoys solid discussions: likes to dance now and then, but usually prefers sitting on the sidelines to watch.

You will find that he responds to your moods: happy when you are enjoying yourself, moody when you are depressed. Try to be pleasant and agreeable, avoiding unpleasant topics and heavy discussions. He is too discerning to be susceptible to open flattery, but appreciates subtly expressed approval, if he honestly feels it justified, of his intellectual capacities and accomplishments. You will find him pretty firm about the things he cherishes deeply, such as conventions, family traditions, value of education and the like: you will be wise to find what these convictions are and cater to them.

THINGS TO AVOID WITH CANCER MEN

Don't attempt to dominate him.
Avoid extravagance, and interference of relatives.
Be conservative and unostentatious in manner: avoid exaggerated make-up and dress.
Avoid a full social calendar. Let *him* make the plans.

TO ATTRACT AND PLEASE A LEO WOMAN

Your Leo woman loves flattery, and the best form of it is lots of attention. She enjoys basking in social popularity, and the little courtesies mean much to her: you must never forget to mark her birthdays, anniversaries, Valentine's Day and Easter, and especially the little sentimental dates you share with her alone.

She loves surprises. The absurd impractical gift means much more to her than "something for the

93

house," for what she prizes is the sentiment of the gift and its evidence that you thought of her. The note, greeting card or telegram of remembrance is a "gift" in her eyes. If you are parted from her, write often and in endearing terms.

Though, like Leo Norma Shearer, she may carry on a career, at heart she is a home body. She is generous, loves to have her dear ones about her at holidays. She enjoys cooking for you, and most of her pleasures center about the house. Spend lots of time with her at home: go window-shopping with her, chat about the planning and furnishing of the house you may share someday. She wants to be a pal as well as a sweetheart, sharing your problems, sorrows and joys. She is thrifty, knows how to save money, and you can well listen to her advice concerning your business and financial affairs.

She is not coy, and has no false modesty or reticence, so you can discuss your love openly. She is honest and sincere: though her physical magnetism gives her some slight inclination to flirt, it is harmless. She knows how to be true and loyal to her mate.

THINGS TO AVOID WITH LEO WOMEN

Don't criticize her clothes, friends, personality or home.

Keep away from religious discussions and family questions.

HOW TO ATTRACT THE ONE YOU LOVE

Don't try to dominate her: guard against forcing your own opinions, friends, sports, and preferences.

Don't nag or quarrel. Since she resents evasiveness, always be frank and outspoken.

TO ATTRACT AND PLEASE A LEO MAN

Your typical Leo man is self-confident, proud, and apt to be a bit boastful.

Give his ego something to feed on. It flatters him to be made much over, though you mustn't betray your anxiety to win him at too early a stage. He is intrigued by aloofness and mystery, and will like you better if he thinks he has to pursue you. Since he likes to feel that he is conquering you, don't be too aggressive or forward.

Naturally, he is a dominating type. But let him feel that he is privileged in being permitted to share his confidences with you: don't do too much of the talking yourself, let him set the mood and pace. Follow his lead, being somewhat on the passive and negative side.

He is frank and open: no coyness or false modesty about him. When your romance is well-established, be yourself with him: show your affection, and don't be prudish. Let him know that you love the home and children, that you like his family and friends; sympathize in his problems, and take an interest in his business or career. But mean what you say, be-

95

cause he has an intuitive sense that warns him of insincerity.

He is generally well-liked, and women especially find him charming and attractive. Cheerful and sociable, you can appeal to him through his sense of fun and humor, though you must be prepared to take without hurt his satirical turn of phrase: he means no offense by it.

THINGS TO AVOID WITH LEO MEN

Don't drink, smoke, chew gum or indulge in other personal habits if he resents them: he will tell you his feelings frankly.

Refrain from talking too much about yourself, your work, your friends, especially about the men you know: he likes to hold the center of the stage.

Don't flirt too openly with other men, and never try deliberately to excite his jealousy.

Admit his domination, and don't force him to go to places or do things which he doesn't care for. He has an especial dislike of being discussed or criticized in company.

TO ATTRACT AND PLEASE A VIRGO WOMAN

Your Virgo woman is practical, and though unusually adaptable, she nevertheless has certain strong preferences which you should study.

She has an appreciation of money and the things

it will buy, but she by no means worships it. Financial success means to her not so much money as the visible, material proof of accomplishment. Let her know that you are eager to get ahead in the world; that you are using your time to develop yourself and your talents.

Virgo is ruled by Mercury, the planet which governs the mind. She admires anyone who is intellectual and well read. Her tastes are more classical than modern in the arts, and you can expect her to enjoy opera, serious music, and great literature.

She is idealistic, and likes to be able to look up to anyone she loves. She won't demand all your time and attention, for she is very understanding: when in love, she will enjoy exerting a motherly and protective interest over your life.

Once her confidence is won, she is exceptionally easy to get along with. Once in a while her desire for faultless perfection (remember, she wants to look up to you) may be irritating; but you must overlook it, and try to meet her wishes. Along this line, she may be somewhat critical of mistakes you make, especially in grammar and conduct: she resents little personality traits and mannerisms which might cause friction, and she may even demand that you constantly change your personality to fit a mental phase through which she happens to be passing at the moment.

She makes a wonderful companion. She likes outdoor sports and recreation, but adapts herself to social life with ease and success.

Things to Avoid with Virgo Women

Shun temperamental outbursts: she admires calm and poise.

Don't resent her criticisms, for she is working toward perfection for herself as well as you.

Refrain from making decisions without consulting her; she likes to advise, and feel that she is useful to you.

Don't attempt to pry into her personal life if she seems at all reluctant to reveal it.

Remember that kindness and sympathy mean much more to her than luxurious and expensive gifts.

TO ATTRACT AND PLEASE A VIRGO MAN

This Sign possesses great executive ability. Your Virgo man can be depended upon for an efficient and capable handling of almost any situation which may arise.

To appeal to him, you must have a nearly perfect personality: combining qualities of tact, determination, poise, charm, and adaptability. This is a big order, but he will demand at least some of each of these qualities in the person he loves.

Outsiders may consider him cold and selfish. He is not, actually: this attitude is simply a reasoned conservation of his energies. He wisely knows he cannot mend everything that is wrong with the world, so he wastes no time in pity and talk, but acts in a practical way to help generously those close to him whom he loves. Don't misjudge this misleadingly callous exterior, and don't try to make him act against his reasoned convictions.

Appeal to his sense of fairness in all things, for he is honorable and just: his decisions are generally the result of calm, mature judgment. Let him choose the places to go and people to see. He likes to "father" his loved ones, so let him feel that you are leaning on him.

His instincts are strong, and you can well be guided by them. Honor and respect his parents, for he loves them dearly. He adores children and pets, but his sense of order and system demands that they be kept in their proper places.

THINGS TO AVOID WITH VIRGO MEN

Don't intrude with talk when he seems silent and thoughtful.

Avoid confusion and discord, for he places a high value on peace and harmony. Don't nag him about little things, and never cry over spilt milk: he will be highly irritated at the waste of energy.

Wait until he calms down before questioning his decisions.

Avoid extremes in anything, of the inner emotions

as well as the externals: he likes a reasoned moderation.

Don't indulge in personal habits or mannerisms for which he expresses or implies distaste.

TO ATTRACT AND PLEASE A LIBRA WOMAN

This Sign is ruled by the planet of romance and beauty, Venus. Your Libra woman is therefore inclined to be artistic, creative, and romantic.

Act the part of a romantic hero brought up to date, a sort of D'Artagnan in modern dress and mind, and she will probably love it. She likes finery, beautiful clothes and jewelry especially: perfumes, exquisite gifts, antiques all appeal to her tremendously.

You will find her discriminating, and in spite of her romantic tendencies, a trifle cynical in outlook. Your first approach must be cautious and delicate. She will resent familiarity on first acquaintance, and does not like anyone who is forward and aggressive. Treat her always with tact and diplomacy.

She will like you to be orderly and precise in your habits. She admires punctuality, and resents broken promises. It will be wise of you to remember such important events as her birthday and holidays: also, if you get that far, her anniversary.

She herself, however, is a temperamental creature. She acts on impulses and is apt to get angry over things you unwittingly do. When the storms come, the wisest course is to let her alone until she cools down.

Things to Avoid with Libra Women

Gentle persuasion is better than attempts to order her about.

Don't let yourself be quarrelsome or speak sharply: she loves a peaceful atmosphere, on your part at least.

Don't force her to accompany you in outdoor sports, for she has no strong inclination for them.

Don't preach economy to her. Avoid discussions of business and politics.

If you dislike music, art, and literature, don't let her know about it: set about cultivating these tastes.

TO ATTRACT AND PLEASE A LIBRA MAN

Your typical Libra man is a good fellow: apt to be hasty tempered, a bit unconventional, and one who greatly enjoys social popularity.

Frankly, he tends to admire beauty of face and figure more than intelligence in women. He loves the good, earthy things of life—good food and drink, good clothes, fine homes and expensive cars. His tastes are excellent, not garish. In spite of his liking for surface attractiveness, however, he likes women to be capable, independent, and sensible.

He responds to love. Cater to his vanity, flatter him on occasion, admire his intellect and possessions. He likes money and the things it will buy: if you can give him really good advice and encouragement concerning his future career he will appreciate it, but you must let him be cock-of-the-walk on all final decisions.

Generally speaking, you will find him amiable, affectionate, and of cheerful disposition, though his moods may fluctuate with his personal fortunes, or even with the weather. His essential aggressiveness is somewhat tempered by the romantic touch of Venus, and he is an idealist in romance, easily disillusioned in the one he loves.

Libra is represented by the Scales. He is always weighing both sides of every question, deciding for or against something or somebody. You can always appeal to his reason with the assurance of getting a just and impartial decision in vital matters. Don't force him to change his mind once it is made up.

He is not easily won, for he is very popular with women. Once yours, however, you can hold him indefinitely if you understand and sympathize with his inner character.

THINGS TO AVOID WITH LIBRA MEN

Don't flirt or let your affections seem to vacillate: he likes to feel that he possesses your whole heart.

Don't be a mental sluggard: satisfy his admiration for keen wit and intelligence.

Avoid any appearance of bossing him, and don't force him to introduce you to all his friends.

HOW TO ATTRACT THE ONE YOU LOVE

TO ATTRACT AND PLEASE A SCORPIO WOMAN

This Sign is ruled by Mars, and women born in Scorpio are exceptionally aggressive, dynamic, and forceful in personality.

She will have little use for a weakling. To appeal to her inner nature, you must be a fighter, tackling every problem as though it were a matter of life or death, never accepting defeat in anything. She likes money and is willing to admit it: she recognizes that everyone has to start somewhere, but will admire you only if you are working hard to become a financial success.

You must focus all your energies on her and her life. She likes concentrated attention, and the more solicitous you are of her and her welfare, the deeper will be the impression you make.

Though mental and spiritual in character, she has a streak of earthiness. She is emotional, and sometimes lets her emotions run away with her. Pleasantly, she will respond with ardent demonstration of affection: on the other hand, her displeasure is shown by stinging rebukes which you can't easily forget. To conquer a Scorpio woman you must be able to "take it" without being crushed. Remember always that she says more in anger than she really means: knowing this, you can forgive her outbursts and adopt the wise course of acting as though nothing had happened.

Your own and her standing in the community, and with your group of friends, mean much to her. In fact, she values even the opinion of complete strangers, and is ruled by her fear of "what people will say." Remember this, and even though you may disagree, be governed by her feelings.

THINGS TO AVOID WITH SCORPIO WOMEN

Don't be sarcastic or cynical, even though she may.
Don't show discouragement or inclination to give up a struggle.
Avoid moodiness and depression: she likes cheerful persons.
Don't appear penurious, for she resents any appearance of stinginess, especially in the presence of others.

TO ATTRACT AND PLEASE A SCORPIO MAN

Scorpio is ruled by the fighting planet Mars. However, your Scorpio man is generally peaceful in nature until roused by persistent opposition.

He is patient and long-suffering, willing to stand an astounding amount of abuse from the one he loves. Your pitfall is in taking advantage of this. Be warned that he eventually reaches a saturation point, and then turns with bitter Scorpio fury on his unfortunate victim. His fury has tremendous staying powers, and he will wait for days to get square with you for your mistakes.

Treat him with continuous deference and respect, however, and you will win his undying friendship and affection. He is very intelligent, and is most considerate of the one he loves. Treat him with kindness and love, and he will do anything you wish.

He is ardent, emotional, and sentimental. Take notice, however, that he often lets these emotions degenerate into sensuality. If this offends you, overcome his tendencies gradually and tactfully, subtly teaching him self-control. This sensuality is fortunately confined to the one he loves, for his innate sense of honesty keeps him in the straight and narrow path of love. He does not like to break off a romance, and once his love is won you can keep him almost indefinitely.

Encourage his career, and take a keen interest in his work. He likes to hear your advice, whether or not he follows it. But it must always be advice, not command: he wants to take the active lead. He enjoys dominating you, but he can be fooled rather easily if you give in to him on the numerous small issues which arise, making your stand on important matters.

THINGS TO AVOID WITH SCORPIO MEN

Don't deny him plenty of affection.

Avoid involved situations with relatives, and don't expect him to be a social butterfly: he dislikes formal affairs especially.

Don't seem too positive: especially don't insist that he study something which he dislikes.

TO ATTRACT AND PLEASE A SAGITTARIUS WOMAN

Your Sagittarius woman is capable, independent, and in no sense a clinging vine. She is probably making her own living in the business world, and perhaps supporting relatives.

Romance is an escape from reality for her. She dreams of a Prince Charming who is gentle, courteous and chivalrous. Essentially feminine despite her economic independence, she thrills at the small attentions: likes you to help her on and off with her coat, hold doors for her, assist her in and out of cars, and so on—all the old-fashioned deferences which went out with the War. Underneath her veneer of capability she is sensitive and emotional: very easily hurt, you must not offend or alarm her with brusqueness.

She is progressive and intelligent. Perhaps she is making more money than you are at the moment: if that is so, don't be ashamed of it, for she will appreciate your ambition and your willingness to work to get ahead.

Your affection for her should not be shown in public except in those small courtesies, for she resents ostentation and demonstrativeness. In private, however, she wants your affection. Though not a moral prude—quite modern, in fact, about such matters as eugenics and birth control—she believes very strongly in the sanctity of marriage. She wants the one love of her life to lead to a permanent marriage, with a home and children of her own.

THINGS TO AVOID WITH SAGITTARIUS WOMEN

Don't urge her to give up her career: leave the choice up to her.

Don't flirt with other women.

Avoid an active social life if she doesn't care for it.

Don't be dictatorial about how she should dress, wear her hair, furnish her home, or other things which she considers her personal province.

TO ATTRACT AND PLEASE A SAGITTARIUS MAN

Your Sagittarius man is a sentimentalist, and his first real sweetheart always keeps a hold on his affections.

He is easy to win, but not easy to hold. It is especially necessary for you to know his inner likes and dislikes so that you may make yourself exactly what he wants in a woman.

He is moody, easily depressed, and is helped by an unobtrusive cheerfulness in you. Intellectually alert, his mind works overtime: he tires easily, and you must never force him to exert himself strenuously when he desires rest. He hates detail; dislikes people who talk boringly of themselves.

Large gatherings of people are distasteful to him: he especially resents an atmosphere of confusion in the home. However, he enjoys dancing, and likes small parties where he can concentrate on you.

He is susceptible to attractive clothes, and has an eye for rich fabrics and smart design. If you can't afford to spend much on clothes, it's better to buy just a few dresses and to have them expensive and smart. He likes plain jewelry, simple hairdress, and inconspicuous makeup.

His attitude toward love and marriage is old fashioned. Whatever he himself may do, he demands that the girl he marries be chaste. Pre-marital intimacy is the surest way to lose his respect, regardless of what he may say at the moment. You can win him over by being modest, sweet-tempered, gentle, and sympathetic. Take an interest in his work and home. Cultivate a liking for his relatives; let him choose the places you go of an evening, dress simply, and let him lead the conversation.

Things to Avoid with Sagittarius Men

Don't insist on working after marriage if he doesn't like the idea.

Drop any undesirable friends, for he is apt to judge you by the company you keep.

HOW TO ATTRACT THE ONE YOU LOVE

Observe his wishes about plans for engagement, marriage, and the home. Keep your relatives out of your affairs, and don't nag or criticize.

TO ATTRACT AND PLEASE A CAPRICORN WOMAN

This Sign is ruled by Saturn, the planet of obstacles.

Your Capricorn girl is complex and hard to understand. She is quiet and serious at heart: you cannot force your attentions on her at first meeting, and shouldn't try.

Don't be discouraged if at first she seems stubborn and evasive, for this is a mask she presents to people she has not yet admitted inside the walls of her natural reserve. The courtship must be longer than usual, since she needs a long time to make up her mind in vital matters. But there is no indecisiveness in her nature—she either likes you a great deal or not at all. Once her love is won you will find her gentle, patient, and most generous.

She is generally musical, artistic and creative. Take an interest in the things she enjoys. The best date is a trip: a long drive to the country, a boat trip, or an excursion to some place of scenic beauty. Though she can mix socially and is admired by others, she likes best being alone with the one she loves.

You will find her an idealist, and should respect her fine sensibilities in romance. She frowns upon unconventionality, and keenly resents such "modern" institutions as free love, companionate marriage, and easy divorce. She is a home lover; fond of children; inclined to hobbies which develop the home instinct and accord with her qualities of industry, thrift and conservativeness.

She is easily led when she loves you, so make your plans for marriage with courage and confidence. However, there is a strain of determination and aggressiveness in her character which may lead to clashes over trivial things: so study her likes and dislikes, then respect her wishes and avert quarrels and discord.

THINGS TO AVOID WITH CAPRICORN WOMEN

Don't try to make her give up her friends: avoid any show of jealousy.

Keep to yourself any irritating remarks about her personality and personal habits.

Don't "rush" her: respect her reserves.

TO ATTRACT AND PLEASE A CAPRICORN MAN

The element of secrecy plays a big part in the life of your Capricorn man.

To win and hold him, you can well assume a veil of mystery yourself. Even a touch of aloofness is useful, for he likes to pursue rather than be pursued. Be hard to get and hard to hold: an occasional lover's spat will help rather than harm, provided you don't carry it too far. In other words, be hard to get, but not completely out of reach. His affections are usually permanent when once aroused.

He is apt to have more than one woman in his life at a time, but so shrouded in secrecy is he that you may never find out the real truth about his past, or even his present. Capricorn represents the dark and rather moody section of the Zodiac, so don't expect him to be scintillating with wit and good humor. He is more likely to be moody, introspective, and ultra-conservative. Like the iceberg, the biggest part of his nature is hidden below the surface.

He is an astute business man, and demands that you be well posted on matters of finance and what is going on in the business world. If you keep up with the times, reading substantial books and magazines, you will have enough conversational material to hold his interest and elicit his respect. Being practical, he resents waste of time: he will admire you especially if you have a well thought-out program in life and adhere to it. An honest liking for intellectual things, for art and music, will please him.

He is unusually loyal and sentimental about family. Any dislike you may have for his people is better left unmentioned. You can always appeal to the practical side of his nature: in any argument, present the practical reasons to justify your position, and he will admit their validity without rancor or unfairness.

THINGS TO AVOID WITH CAPRICORN MEN

Don't try to pry into his secret reserves.

Avoid attempts to force the social graces upon him if he prefers his natural taciturnity.

Don't try to make him over: if you can't take him 'as is,' better let the whole thing drop.

TO ATTRACT AND PLEASE AN AQUARIUS WOMAN

This sign is one of the most spiritual and highly developed in the Zodiac.

Your Aquarius woman is marked for fame, if her environment gives any encouragement: in any event, she has latent qualities of genius. Remember that and take it into account when she disturbs you with her eccentricities or unaccountable behavior.

Mentally she is generally stable and poised, always knowing just about where she is going. Yet in romance she is easily swayed: affectionate and demonstrative.

Nevertheless, she is not easily won. She will never throw herself at your feet, for she is outwardly cold and aloof. She requires much wooing, and it may take you a long time to break down her outward reserve. Even then your time will be wasted unless you are her equal in personality, intellect, and universal scope of understanding.

Once inside that barrier of reserve, you will find her charming, sociable, humorous, intellectual, and magnetic. She is usually surrounded by a circle of ardent admirers and friends. You will be fortunate in winning her attentions, for she is a rich personality who gives freely of her special qualities.

Her interests are numerous. She is very much in tune with the times, and to be able to converse intelligently with her you must keep well up on current topics and the trends in the arts.

You must be honestly sincere, unaffected, and agreeable, to appeal to her. Argument, discord, and friction distress her and she will not tolerate such an atmosphere. She would rather meet you half way than to dominate or be dominated. She will be impressed most with your ideas if they are progressive and idealistic.

THINGS TO AVOID WITH AQUARIUS WOMEN

Don't be old fashioned in your views.

Avoid dictation as to her dress and conduct; don't argue in public with her, or with others in her presence.

Don't impose your relatives upon her unless she welcomes them: let her keep her friends.

YOU AND THE STARS

Count on having to go half way with your typical Aquarius man.

You will probably have to make most of the advances, for he is essentially passive in nature. He dreams great dreams, but does not always put them into action. You must be confident of your ability to attract and hold him, for he responds to confidence and assurance in the people with whom he is connected.

The sign of Aquarius rules the mind and the mystic forces. Mould yourself to him and his life, for only by so doing can you be absolutely in tune with his highly spiritual nature. He will not accept your out and out domination, but your suggestions and tactful guidance will be welcomed.

At times the ruling planet Uranus causes these persons to be seriously misunderstood. Though his motives often seem shrouded in mystery, you must not demand explanations which he does not offer. His friendship is delicate as a flower; even small misunderstandings hurt him and send him into his shell. In spite of his cool exterior, he is highly emotional inwardly; it is quite possible that you might possess his love without realizing it. He likes to make gifts, and you should accept them. Incidentally, he can't mix friendship with business: he isn't up to handling the practical and difficult relations of business dealings with a personal friend.

THINGS TO AVOID WITH AQUARIUS MEN

Avoid argument and infringing upon his privacy.

Don't become involved with other persons; but don't show jealousy of his involvements.

Don't take offense at his frequently cryptic remarks.

TO ATTRACT AND PLEASE A PISCES WOMAN

This Sign is ruled by Neptune, the planet of psychic and intuitive powers.

Your Pisces woman has a strange, magnetic power of attraction. You will find yourself intrigued by her without ever knowing exactly why.

A key to her character is her intense fear of poverty, and hatred of being financially dependent upon the charity of strangers. Underneath any other appeal you may have, she will want to be satisfied that you are intelligent, ambitious and industrious: that you can probably take good care of her.

She will like to lean on you, so be sympathetic, encouraging, and strong. Flattery, even if she says she dislikes it, means much to her: she especially likes compliments to her mental abilities and wit, though like any woman a good word for her looks and dress never comes amiss. To win her, you will have to become involved in her life, guiding her scattering efforts into intelligent channels and showing her that you are a true friend as well as a lover.

She is fond of the society of others: likes to talk a lot and make plans for the future. Her mental interests are wide, and if her education encourages her at all, she has a special leaning for business problems and procedures.

You can probably attract her quite easily. She is impressionable: in fact, a little too easily impressed by surface characteristics—the showy personality, the obvious wealth, notable social position, and so on. She is fair game for the "man of the world." See what you have to offer along these lines, and high light them on early acquaintance. Later on, however, you will have to come down to the more solid virtues, if you are to hold her: honesty, intelligence, and thrifty industry.

She is loyal in love, and will fight fiercely for you when the occasion arises. Her nature is sincere and emotional: you can expect quick jealousy and suspicion of any other women in your life. She likes things of the home, and takes a special pleasure in planning the one which you may some day share together.

THINGS TO AVOID WITH PISCES WOMEN

Don't force her to concentrate too long on any one thing: she tires easily of sustained effort, and likes change.

Avoid carelessness about matters of dress and conduct, but don't quarrel with her over trifles.

Don't monopolize the conversation: she likes to express herself freely.

Avoid unconventionality, out of respect for her leaning to the old-fashioned virtues.

Don't restrict her on the ground that she is a woman: she believes very strongly in equality of the sexes.

TO ATTRACT AND PLEASE A PISCES MAN

Appeal to your Pisces man by the age-old device of seeming very feminine and helpless.

He enjoys the feeling that you depend on his strong shoulders for help in all your problems. Let him counsel you on your business and financial affairs, give you sage advice on your problems of personality, family troubles, and friends. He is easily flattered by small attentions, and you can almost always get him in a melting mood by letting him see how big and strong you think him.

As a matter of fact, he is a very competent and well-rounded man. Pisces has made him artistic and creative, and his inborn aptitude for commercial affairs gives him an excellent balance. You will find him forceful, magnetic, and compelling: very hard to resist.

He likes the simple life. Though he is perfectly at home in society, he really prefers quieter surroundings which cater to his home instincts. He likes to make plans for your future together, and you can count on his being sincere.

If he says he loves you, he usually means it, for he inclines to know intuitively when he has found the right girl. He won't bother to dissimulate: if he feels you have nothing in common, he is apt to tell you so quite frankly.

He is attractive to other women, and you can expect keen competition. Usually, by the way, his magnetism lies in his eyes, his most attractive features. He knows how to make love, you will discover, but he is also an idealist. He likes affection, but not in public. Actually, he's a decided sentimentalist, and you can have your way with him almost always if you are tactful, peaceful, and kind.

Things to Avoid with Pisces Men

Don't try to cajole flattery from him: he's too sincere for that.

Avoid hurrying him, especially in business matters.

Remember that his little attentions to other women mean nothing, and don't be jealous.

Don't be impatient or unkind about his mistakes, and don't provoke him over little things.

★ 5 ★

NEW JOY IN MARRIAGE

DIVORCE is the public confession of a tragic mistake.

The grounds for a divorce may be listed on the court records as incompatibility, infidelity, cruelty, or any of a hundred others. These are actually effects, not causes.

The true cause of a broken marriage is the failure of two people to understand each other, to recognize the planetary compulsions of innate character under which each is being driven.

Such failure is needless.

Marriage is the biggest thing in life to most of us. Perhaps you are finding your partnership disagreeable or drab. If so, take heart, for I can assure you that you can find new joy in marriage, if you will seek it earnestly and intelligently.

Let these pages start you thinking analytically about your marriage; perhaps for the first time, since most Signs are prone to act on impulse or emotion rather than deep thought and reasoning. Search your own character. Search that of your mate, finding the star-given compulsions by which each of you is motivated. See Why each of you acts as you do. Then, in the light of this new knowledge, adapt and mould yourself accordingly, finding a harmony and happiness in your relationship which you had never realized it could hold.

In Chapter 2, I told you which Signs are by nature compatible and incompatible to yours. If you have not yet married, you will do well to take the path of least resistance, choosing a mate whose star-given character harmonizes naturally with yours. That, to borrow a phrase from the sporting gentry, is simply playing the percentages. But in case you have already fallen in love with or married a person whose Sign is incompatible, remember what I went on to say in that same chapter. No person on earth is *absolutely* incompatible to you: there is no adverse destiny, no trait of character, no natural incompatibility, which cannot be overcome, provided you *know* what you must fight, and then fight it with all the illimitable resources of the human mind and spirit.

Human nature doesn't change much with time. Therefore, if you are facing a marriage problem, even though you have been married for many years, re-read Chapter 4 also. Though it deals with Courtship, your mate still has those same traits in romance, those same likes and dislikes. And I might add that once you learn to carry the feeling of courtship over into marriage, half your problems are solved before they arise. That is old stuff. But it's good stuff, too. That is why it's old.

In this chapter I want to discuss those traits of your character which are brought out by the day-to-day intimate association of marriage. Study your own sign, to learn of the traits which you should perhaps adjust or correct. Then study with even more care the sign of your mate, to learn the traits to which you must adjust yourself, and for which perhaps you must make allowances. A careful comparison of the two inner characters will show you just where friction in the close association of marriage is most apt to arise. A pitfall loses most of its danger when you know in advance that it exists.

While I have no desire to deliver an essay on marriage, I do want to give you some basic suggestions. They are simply common-sense rules. They have in common with Astrology only the fact that in the thousands of domestic difficulties which I have had professional occasion to investigate, the real causes of the trouble all came back to these things.

After marriage, you may be "one flesh." You will never be "one mind." Your mate still thinks of himself as an individual. Recognize that, and grant him the small rights and liberties which he must retain to protect his self-respect. Don't demand that every smallest thought and interest be shared. Give him (or her) the priceless privilege of privacy, one small corner of his mind where he can be himself alone.

Keep the "mystery." Never let your mate feel that you are completely understood, entirely possessed. Part of your allure during courtship was the fact that he was curious about you, both mentally and physically. Don't ever let his curiosity be sated. Once a book has been fully read, the temptation is strong to pick up another. This, if you will forgive me, applies especially to matters of physical modesty in matters of dress, toilette, and personal habits.

Be patient. Rome wasn't built in a day, but most married people try to correct the faults of their mates in even less time than that. It's a long life, and you've plenty of time to work. True, you can't permit, for example, the same domination under which you bowed cheerfully during courtship, but you can try to overcome it bit by bit. Oddly, the same person who would drive his car around a Detour sign on a highway as a matter of course, tries to batter and smash his way straight through any obstacle of character. Try detouring.

Treat your wife with the same courtesy you do your secretary. Show your husband the same consideration you accord your servants. And use these as your watchwords: Tact, subtlety, patience, tolerance, understanding, and forbearance.

NEW JOY IN MARRIAGE

Getting back to Astrology and its place in your life, the greatest of these words is *understanding*. Search, as I have told you, your own character. Delve into the true hidden character of your mate. Find how he thinks, what hidden compulsions drive him, why he acts as he does. And as a reward, you will suddenly find a new joy in marriage.

After studying the Signs, ask yourself these two questions; and be honest with yourself in answering them. Does your character clash with any of his deep-rooted traits? Do you fail to satisfy any of his star-given desires? Then figure out calmly what you can do about it.

HAPPINESS IN MARRIAGE WITH
AN ARIES WOMAN

Your Aries wife is very apt to be dominating; often hard to understand and get on with for that reason.

Though this Sign represents the intellectual and spiritual planes of expression, your Aries wife can be very earthy and stubborn on occasion. She is naturally a dominating type, and will create unpleasant situations if you attempt to order her about.

She will particularly resent your domination (which she will call "interference") in matters concerning the home and children, which she rightly considers her province. But you must insist, however gently, that she allow you to manage your end of things, the business and finance. Never steamroller her into acceding to your wishes: appeal to her sense of logic and fairness.

Fortunately, she makes an excellent mother and cares for her home efficiently. She has a good money sense, and can be trusted with a household allowance and charge accounts. In fact, though you cannot permit her to run your business, yet you will do well to consult her and consider her suggestion on your investments.

You will find her sentimental and affectionate. She will enjoy your companionship. In fact, she will probably resent your evenings out, though you can subtly overcome this by encouraging her to seek her own friends and amusements. It's only common sense for married people to retain their own individualities by having the freedom to go out alone now and then.

Beware of exciting her jealousy or suspicion. It's even unwise to be too nice to her women friends. She herself enjoys male attention, but her nature is so honorable that she sees no harm in it, and will quite unreasonably resent any show of jealousy on your part.

In raising children Aries is an exacting mother, but a patient and considerate one. You may even find it necessary to gently correct her tendency to spoil the children with too much attention. Since her mind functions best under peaceful conditions, avoid any confusion and excitement in the home. If an emergency arises, treat it calmly.

HAPPINESS IN MARRIAGE WITH AN ARIES MAN

Your Aries man is—no other word for it—bossy.

He wants his own way always. If he doesn't get it, you can expect him to be depressed, hurt, or to burst into a fit of temper. Mars rules this sign, and it gives your husband a chip-on-the-shoulder attitude. He is apt to contradict or criticize everything you say or do, and you must learn early in your marriage to ride the storms. Fighting back or flaring up simply makes matters worse. Though very possibly your Aries husband has schooled himself into controlling this part of his nature, it is nevertheless there and must be reckoned with.

He is apt to be, also, rather vain and conceited. You can therefore count on his responding to flattery, kindness and sentiment: which, in fact, is probably the best way to overcome or prevent the storms mentioned above.

You must encourage him in thrifty habits, for he has a tendency to spend more than he makes in "keeping up with the Joneses." Even in business, he may assume obligations which seriously impede his financial progress. This you can overcome by bringing out the positive side of these lavish qualities. He likes a home of his own, the best of everything for himself and his family, and can be encouraged to save for such goals. He is admirably industrious, capable and intelligent, with consuming ambition. You must encourage him in his work, buoy him on to greater things, and never permit him to settle back into a rut of self-complacency.

Your Aries husband likes children, pets, gardening. The bigger your family, the better he will like it and the harder he will work for them. Despite his dominating nature, he is easy to handle if you approach him reasonably and in good humor, respecting his rights and liberties.

He is seldom disloyal to his mate. If, however, he should happen to stray, keep cool and handle the situation with all the diplomacy you can muster. Raising a fuss will be fatal: it will only bring matters to a head and call in that stubbornness of his. Pretend, if possible, that you don't know what is going on: if you must admit your knowledge, pretend indifference, for any excitement on your part will simply make the other woman important in his mind. Left to himself, he will forget her. Don't give him up without a fight, because he is worth fighting for.

NEW JOY IN MARRIAGE

HAPPINESS IN MARRIAGE WITH A
TAURUS WOMAN

Your Taurus woman is very affectionate. She wants constant reassurance and demonstration of your love, expects the marriage ceremony to be the beginning of one long honeymon. She is sentimental about such things as her home, friends, and relatives: expects you to remember and mark the birthdays, anniversaries, and sentimental occasions.

The home means much to her. Her sign is the productive Earth, and she is generally happy to be the mother of at least two children for the man she loves. She is a real home-builder, and expects you to coöperate. Allied to this is her sense of thrift, and her resentment of extravagance and wasteful habits in you.

She may be jealous, somewhat possessive, and quite aggressive. Expecting her marriage to last for life, she will be much upset by any light attitude toward it on your part. You must not try to dominate her, but win her over by gentle persuasion. She will respond to affection, and you can remould her character by tactful and patient effort. Depend on her sense of fairness.

A Taurus woman is generally physically attractive, and the years seldom dim her essential youth and beauty. She has, however, a tendency to become careless in the security of marriage about her figure and appearance: you must subtly encourage her in keeping her attractiveness.

HAPPINESS IN MARRIAGE WITH A TAURUS MAN

Your Taurus man must feel that he is the boss in his family.

Nevertheless, he has some bad tendencies which, for the protection of yourself and your home, you must subtly try to correct. He likes card-games, and is prone to become a reckless gambler. He is lavish with money, and sometimes throws it away with tragic carelessness. He likes things of the earth, especially good food and drink, and is inclined to overindulge in both.

A constant unobtrusive watchfulness may prevent excesses in any of these things. Flattery will keep him in a sweet and amenable mood. The device of engaging his interest in something sufficiently stimulating to keep him looking forward to it from one day to the next is usually successful.

He will resent interference from you in his business affairs. He prides himself on being a good provider for his family, and will be deeply offended by aspersions on his ability and intelligence. Any nagging, harsh criticism, whining, or show of hopeless outlook drives him to anger. Seem enthused when he suggests something, even though you know you may have to oppose it later when the atmosphere is more suitable.

He is jealous. Loyal and sincere, he expects you to be the same. His home, children, and friends mean much to him, though he doesn't want you to accompany him on purely masculine excursions, such as hunting trips. Divorce is to him a last resort, to which he is driven only by extreme mental incompatibility, infidelity, or interference of relatives. He will welcome a reconciliation after a separation if given a chance.

HAPPINESS IN MARRIAGE WITH A
GEMINI WOMAN

Your Gemini wife is the essence of charm. She knows all the alluring little things which men like, and if she has carried over her courtship personality into marriage, you are a very fortunate and happy individual.

You are also, however, a busy one. She loves lots of friends, and craves a very active social life: to such an extent that you may find her hard to keep up with. She can be brilliant, witty and affectionate: but she can also make herself very uncomfortable to get along with.

She is possessive, inclined to jealousy, and quick

to suspicion. Being also clever and intuitive, she will see through any untrue excuse on your part. She herself is somewhat flirtatious, but she is trustworthy and loyal and means nothing by her little escapades.

She will manage your home well, though not economically. She is lavish and extravagant by nature, and likes to outshine the neighbors. You may be exasperated at times by her apparent belief that your financial resources are bottomless, a belief which no amount of argument will entirely overcome. Unless she inherited enough business sense from her parents to combat this phase of her stargiven nature, you will have to block off trouble before it arises by taking extra precautions with regard to household allowances and charge accounts. Though she will enjoy giving advice in your business and financial affairs, it will seldom be sound. She is a driver, and expects you to make good in your business.

Gemini often marries twice, but if you are halfway compatible, she will stand much. Though she loves children, this is seldom a fertile sign and you will probably not have more than one or two children, if indeed any at all.

NEW JOY IN MARRIAGE

HAPPINESS IN MARRIAGE WITH A GEMINI MAN

You will often think that your Gemini husband is neglectful, even tired of you.

That is probably not true. Astrologically, he has a strong tendency to concentration: his lack of attention to you is simply intense preoccupation with whatever is filling his one-track mind at the moment. Incidentally, don't try to force more than one idea on him at a time: before you advance a new one, be sure the first is digested and out of the way. He likes to throw himself wholeheartedly into his work, and he concentrates on the project in hand to the complete exclusion of everything else.

This tendency to do everything to death evidences itself in other ways. He takes up friends furiously for a few weeks or months, only to forget them as though they had never existed. His sports, hobbies, and other interests are treated in the same manner. You must understand this trait, and allow for it. More than that, you must vary yourself, your personality, your interests, so that he doesn't tire of you.

He will demand a great deal of your time and attention. Though rather aloof in temperament, he will respond to kindness and affection: he appreciates consideration from you in his varying moods.

When quarrels arise, you will be wise to back down, at least until he is in a more reasonable mood, for he likes to feel that he is having his own way. He is almost certain to say biting and sarcastic things which will be very hard for you to stand, but keep calm by reminding yourself that when his storm of temper passes he will be sorry for what he has said, anxious to make up and ask forgiveness. Most Gemini divorces are due to the wife's hasty action, based upon lack of understanding of this inner character.

Your Gemini husband is generous, but not for foolish things. He likes solidity, and generally wants to create a beautiful and substantial home environment. Generally he is the safe type who believes in insurance, annuities, and solid investments; sticking to one job or one line of business. You can trust his judgment in matters of money, and depend upon his fairness.

HAPPINESS IN MARRIAGE WITH A
CANCER WOMAN

Remember always that your Cancer wife comes under the rulership of the changeable Moon.

Her liking for change and variety will definitely affect your life together. You might be content to stay in one place and in one occupation for a long time, but not Cancer. She will be restless and discontented if she cannot change her place of residence every three or four years. In the meantime, she will change the furniture about, redecorate the house, and have a constant stream of relatives and friends passing through her life.

This craving for change gives her a restless mind. Fortunately she is charitable and benevolent, and her mental restlessness can often be worked off through activity in women's clubs, social service projects, and the like. Her advice on your business affairs is not too dependable, since it is apt to be based more on her desire to do something different than on a sound, reasoned consideration of the matter.

She is a good homemaker. She enjoys working around the home, and thrives on the attention of her loved ones. Though somewhat hard to get along with at times, especially when she is bored with what to her is monotony, you must take her as she is and treat her whims with patience and tolerance. Use your ingenuity to invent diversions which will satisfy her desire for change without really upsetting your scheme of life.

She may have friends of whom you do not wholly approve. You will be wise to make no open objection to them, since she will resent it: she will drop them soon anyway. You may find it necessary to insist on your right to your own friends. Quarrels may arise over relatives: your Cancer wife is extremely fond of her own parents, but quite apt to honestly feel that yours are tyrants, bent on mischief. It will require firmness on your part to keep the home intact and free from the interference of relatives on both sides.

HAPPINESS IN MARRIAGE WITH A CANCER MAN

You must learn to accord with your Cancer husband's demands for thrift and system.

He is conservative and cautious in financial matters. Though not penurious, he is nevertheless thrifty and careful about money. He will require that you watch your expenditures and avoid extravagances. He is perfectly willing to spend money on the home, but he insists that any purchase be necessary, within the budget, and carefully considered.

You can please him tremendously if you run your home and personal life on an orderly and systematic basis. Keep notes, write down engagements, list your expenditures, run a budget—all these things satisfy his liking for method, efficiency, and economy of energy. Above all, avoid debt, and don't urge him to any expense which he feels is unwise. When you discuss purchases or expenses, do so in a coöperative manner, honestly searching for the best thing to do.

There is not much danger of disloyalty on his part. He's usually too busy in his work for that. If his affections should stray, you can expect him to be honest about it, and talk the whole matter out very frankly. He will seldom want a divorce for his own sake, but will grant you one if he is satisfied that you will be happier with some other man. In the event of divorce, he will be reasonable and liberal about any settlements.

However, he makes a very affectionate, sincere husband, and is a good provider. He responds to affection, and appreciates your remembering his comforts. He wants good food and a substantial environment: likes children and pets.

You must grant him a certain amount of privacy. He should have a den or study where he can be alone when he wishes. Although he will enjoy suggestions regarding his business affairs, he is apt to feel that you are intruding on his business if you take too active an interest. You can safely leave financial matters up to him; his business judgment is sound, and your future will be well guarded.

HAPPINESS IN MARRIAGE WITH A
LEO WOMAN

This sign is ruled by the Sun and symbolized by the Lion, so expect your Leo wife to be an outstanding person.

She should possess a brilliant and dynamic personality, be witty and clever, and the center of a large circle of friends. Her belief in the equality of women to men is very strong, and if she wishes a career you should not stand in her way: being capable and gifted, she might rise to great heights in the business or artistic world.

However, her chosen career is most likely to be her home. She is very fond of children, and it is wise to have one or two quite early in marriage, since this seems to fully develop the beautiful character so often found among Leo women. She makes a wonderful mother, willing and glad to sacrifice her time and attention to the upbringing of her children.

Being Leo, she is of course inclined to be the leader. You will be wise to let her have full domination over the home and matters connected with it, including her personal friendships. But early in your relationship, make it definitely understood that she is to let you run your business affairs, neither of you trespassing without invitation on the other's territory. She requires a peaceful environment; a thorough understanding in these matters will block off a major source of discord. But consult with her on business affairs, because she has an excellent mind; simply make it clear that she is giving advice, not orders.

She is poised and well-balanced mentally. She seldom overdoes in entertaining, or lavishing money on friends. You will find that she can manage money and save it. Her real worth will be proven when the reverses come, for she will be staunch, loyal, and coöperative through the blackest times. In fact, you have chosen such a worthwhile helpmate that you will have your work cut out for you in living up to her high character and noble qualities.

Though she is fond of compliments, she likes to feel that she has earned them. Flatter her, but make it sincere. She likes more than most women the small remembrances and the little occasional gifts, whether they mark a significant date or not.

You will hear, and it is true, that a surprising number of Leo women find unhappiness in marriage, but this is usually due to their having mated with an incompatible Sign: once compatibly mated, they are more than apt to be happy and contented for life. There is, as I have said, no item of incompatibility between your two signs and inner natures which cannot be overcome with intelligent effort.

HAPPINESS IN MARRIAGE WITH A LEO MAN

You are probably the envy of your friends. Your Leo husband, if his heredity hasn't buried his birthright, is a very attractive individual: well built, with a pleasant smile and personality, sparkling eyes and so on.

Socially, everyone will like him on sight. Living

with him, you will find that he has a less attractive side to his nature. Though ruled by the Sun, and genial most of the time, he is subject to deep shadows: spells of black moodiness and depression. Don't desert him in these periods, for the breach thus created between you may never heal. He is emotional, vacillating, and mentally complex: quite apt to take offense at some word or action of yours and retire behind an impenetrable wall for hours or days at a time. He can overcome these moody spells only if you work with him with the ultimate of patience, kindness, and understanding.

He likes home life and friends. Make it a point to surround him with people he likes: the wider variety the better, including persons from the business, artistic and creative fields. Just as a suggestion, music, soft lights, and attractive surroundings exert a strong influence on the Leo mind.

He will require that you be calm and unruffled on all occasions. Even though you do your own housekeeping, you must greet him when he comes home in the evening as fresh as though you had spent the day resting. He admires neatness, likes you to be dressed in the latest styles. Overdone makeup, dyed hair, and the like are distasteful to him, but he will want you to keep your skin and figure fresh and youthful. Frankly, your Leo husband is a hard man to please: but he is usually well worth the effort.

NEW JOY IN MARRIAGE

HAPPINESS IN MARRIAGE WITH A VIRGO WOMAN

Practical, energetic and capable, Virgo is one of the best Signs from which to select a wife.

If at times you think she is hard driving and insistent, remember that such pressure is generally for your own good. She wants to help you get ahead, as much for your own good as hers. She will never admit defeat, never believe that the man she loves isn't deserving of the greatest things life has to offer. She may even be blind to your weaknesses and mistakes, for Virgo in love overlooks flaws and creates an idealized image which can do no wrong.

She is thrifty by nature. You will find that she is insistent about insurance and protection of all kinds, for she has an intense desire to create a secure future for her loved ones. You will do well to listen to her advice in matters of business—especially those such as questions of partnerships, where your own judgment is clouded by emotion—for she is not only shrewd and practical, but gifted with the ability to look at all sides of a question impersonally. She is, in addition, given to flashes of intuition which are usually dependable: and once she decides on a course of action, she tends to follow it through, regardless of consequences.

Don't expect her to make much fuss over anything,

nor to be sentimentally demonstrative in company. She dislikes ostentation. Given to deeds rather than words, her kindly works are usually done in secret. You will find her strictly loyal. She expects the same loyalty from you, and any unfaithfulness on your part will cause her great agony of mind and spirit: you cannot expect ever to be forgiven. She likes children, and although her Sign is a barren one, there could be at least one child in her life. She will enjoy training such a child with all her attention for some outstanding career, most probably in the arts.

HAPPINESS IN MARRIAGE WITH A VIRGO MAN

You can consider yourself fortunate if you have attracted a Virgo man in marriage. He is intellectual, creative, and very adaptable. These qualities put him in a position to do very well financially.

However, he is more than apt to lose the fruits of his labor in one impulsive speculative venture. You must help him in this respect. Though you may know nothing whatever about the particular investment or venture which he is contemplating, you can persuade him to delay until he has looked the proposition over with great care, free from wishful thinking. He is practical enough to spot the pitfalls if he will only take the time to investigate: your job is to make him take that time.

NEW JOY IN MARRIAGE

Your Virgo husband will not be demonstrative. Actually, he is affectionate and even sentimental. He thinks, however, that a show of such feeling is a weakness, and hides it under a mask of efficiency and practicality. You must recognize that a seemingly casual pat on the cheek is as much a token of affection from him as a kiss would be from another man.

He is, in reality, very much of an idealist. He loves books, art, beautiful music, and enjoys conversation with people who really have something worthwhile to say. In temperament, he is extraordinarily easy-going, and has such a decided hatred of discord that he will stand a great deal. In fact, you must learn to judge from the shadings of his attitude when he is displeased or disapproving; his "yes" if given without enthusiasm probably means "no." Surround him with only a handful of carefully chosen friends, don't force him to attend formal social functions unless he is eager to go, work with him toward a goal which is far ahead of attainment, and you have the ideal formula for happiness in your marriage.

The chances are against his becoming romantically interested in any other woman. He is fastidious: few women interest him, and even then he needs weeks to reach the point of intimacy. Moreover, his mind is usually so concentrated on his work, home, and other interests that he has no time for clandestine amours. He usually stays married, even if only from his distaste of allowing a divorce to interrupt the bustle of his very busy life.

HAPPINESS IN MARRIAGE WITH A
LIBRA WOMAN

The best way to hold the love of your Libra wife is to treat her always as though you were not married to her.

She is in love with love. She will always thrill to the little attentions and amenities you observed during your courtship and honeymoon. You must forever be more the lover than the husband, standing constant guard over her illusions. You may be the type whose comment on the marriage ceremony is, "Well, that's done," thereafter treating her more as a roommate than a mistress: you must mend your ways if you want to maintain marital tranquillity through the long years ahead.

Your Libra wife is an idealist who really works at her trade. She resents and pretends not to see the harsh realities of everyday life, going to great mental lengths to view these realities through rose-colored glasses. So when necessity forces you to shatter one of her illusions, remember her nature and act gently. She is, of course, a sentimentalist: sensitive, intellectual, sociable—a lover of beauty, culture and gentility. If you can harmonize with these qualities, remembering to carry the feeling of courtship over into your marriage, withdrawing when she is moody or pouty, you can pretty well conquer any disturbances which arise in your life together.

She is inclined to be strong-willed, and wants especially to dominate the home. This is her province, so let her hold full sway. However, she is not a typical homebody, and dislikes the work of housekeeping: a maid will add to your harmony when you can afford it. You should sympathize with her liking to have a little social circle around her, and to entertain it at tea, dinner, and bridge. Her unusual ability as a hostess may make her a definite business asset to you. She likes beautiful and fashionable clothes, but her lack of money sense makes it necessary for you to exercise a tactful supervision over her expenditures.

HAPPINESS IN MARRIAGE WITH A LIBRA MAN

So you are married to a Libra husband? Then keep on your toes.

As you undoubtedly have discovered by now, he is often tempted to flirtations with other women. This tendency, given him by his ruling planet Venus, is strong, and you must do two things. First, make allowances for it: ignore his excursions whenever possible, and welcome him back. Second, make yourself so varied and interesting, physically as well as mentally, that he has no compulsion to stray. You must love him enough to take the bitter with the sweet. And there is a lot of sweet, for he is charming, intelligent, a good companion, and has the makings of a successful business man.

He will be particular to the point of fussiness about your appearance. You must not let yourself go. He wants people, and especially his friends, to point you out as being smart, fashionable, attractive, and well groomed. Fortunately, he is willing to pay the price, and will not object to the expense of beauty care, clothes, and so on which another man might class as luxury. The more obviously you fuss about your looks, the better: you can even wear cold cream and beauty masks to bed without objections from him. The surest way to start his eye roving is to be sloppy or neglectful of your appearance. Incidentally, he is equally particular about the appearance of his home.

However, he is not entirely superficial, and you need not fear the approach of age. As he grows older, he appreciates the mental and spiritual qualities more than outward youth or beauty . . . provided only that you are always as smartly turned out as other women of your years. If you progress with a Libra husband, and keep up with his interests, you can hold him forever.

NEW JOY IN MARRIAGE

You will more than once contemplate divorce. Avoid it if at all possible to do so: try patiently to find a way out of your difficulties. If *he* asks for a divorce, stall for time in the well-justified hope that his infatuation for the other woman will wane. In the event of divorce or separation, however, you will find him reasonable, and anxious to see you happy.

HAPPINESS IN MARRIAGE WITH A SCORPIO WOMAN

Remember always that your Scorpio wife is ruled by the fighting planet Mars.

A tremendous force flows through her nature. Exerted positively, she can be a ministering angel. Negatively, she can lash out with a scathing torrent of bitter sarcasm which can cause you great mental distress.

She is generally able to curb this powerful Mars temper, and her normal demeanor is sweet, kind and affectionate. Most outbursts will be short storms, soon over. If she becomes abusive or nagging, it will in all probability be your own fault, the cause being one of two things: the straying of your interest to another woman, or the squandering of carefully-saved money on a spree or some ridiculously foolish expenditure.

Your Scorpio wife is unusually jealous, and will

often suspect you without real cause. Her dislike of extravagance rises from her craving for a financially secure future. Conduct yourself decently and sensibly, and the home will be peaceful except for very little more than the storms which come to any married couple.

She is a good cook and housekeeper: likes children, and makes a kindly, though quite firm, mother. Nature has given her sterling qualities to make up for weakness in temperament. She will never desert you in time of trouble, but gladly work her fingers to the bone to help: Mars lends her tremendous endurance and courage in the face of seemingly overpowering obstacles. She will not seek a divorce or separation except under extreme provocation, and you can best hold her love by being always patient, considerate, and forgiving.

HAPPINESS IN MARRIAGE WITH A SCORPIO MAN

Your Scorpio husband is magnetic, dynamic, and has considerable physical appeal to women. Expect an occasional flirtation. But also expect nothing to come of it unless you drive him into action by opposition.

He is ruled by Mars, and will fight at the drop of a hat, even if he has to drop it himself. He can give worse than he takes, and when he gives an order or takes a stand, he means business. He quite naturally resents any attempt to force him into some action against his will, and is inclined to hold grudges, waiting for days to get square with you for some rebuke or slight.

If you are clever, however, you can keep him tractable and peaceful without giving up your own individuality and desires. Ride the storms without fighting back, saving your side of the question for a more suitable time. Let the small things go by the board without argument, even though you happen to be right. Pamper his liking for his own way by obviously giving in on everything that doesn't matter too much, asking him to give in to you, as a special favor in return, on the few matters which are important to you. In short, be always patient, cautious, and diplomatic.

Your Scorpio mate is by nature a good money maker. Liking the lavish gesture, he may spend more carelessly than you can afford. If you are firm about it you can generally control the family finances, and probably should. He is happiest when surrounded by a gay circle of friends, and a full social schedule is wise. His interest will never wander if you keep him amused and entertained.

HAPPINESS IN MARRIAGE WITH A
SAGITTARIUS WOMAN

You are undoubtedly proud of the charm and intellect of your Sagittarius wife. About certain other qualities, you aren't quite so sure.

Upon coming out of the honeymoon haze, when your every wish was law, she began to take on a quality of determination and domination which shocked and surprised you. Let's analyze this.

Jupiter, her ruling planet, governs business and the home. The combination of these two gives her the strong inclination (and fits her admirably) to hold the reins of the family finances. She wants to handle the home expenses, budget and plan all family expenditures, and will even expect you to hand your entire income over to her and work on a personal allowance. Frankly, she can probably handle these matters better than you, and though your masculine sensibilities may be rather crushed, she will be able to show you good, solid figures at the end of a year to prove that her stewardship was good.

Being highly intelligent and determined, she is not the type to melt or cringe at your approach. She is a fighter, and is grimly determined that her sacred province, the home, shall be under her exclusive domination. If you give her free rein in these matters and do not trespass on her domain, you will not only block off the source of most of your quarrels, but will find a new freedom of mind in the release from petty money matters: you can now put all your time and mental energy on your business.

In some Sagittarius women, this leaning for business leads to an actual business career. If your wife wishes to keep on with her job, you will be wise to agree. Many of these women work in their husbands' businesses, and take orders surprisingly well: they incline to confine their domination to home matters.

Socially, she is an excellent mixer, with a knack for making and keeping friends, and a ready adaptability to any environment. Temperamentally, she is given to outbursts of sarcasm, and can be very unpleasant. But in the home she is neat and orderly: enjoys furnishing and caring for the house, and of course is not given to spending money foolishly. Whatever annoyance you may feel at her bossiness will be balanced by your appreciation of her other qualities: she is unusually loving, affectionate and loyal.

HAPPINESS IN MARRIAGE WITH A SAGITTARIUS MAN

You are proud of your Sagittarius husband and worried about him at the same time.

He is extraordinarily popular. A very nice person, other women flock about him: many people seek out his company, and he has friends by the score. He comes by this popularity naturally, for his nature is charming, magnetic and intellectual. He is a great student of human nature, and really likes people.

But he must be "broken" to marriage, just as a wild horse is broken to harness. The popularity of his bachelorhood may linger in his mind after marriage: he will want to continue spending a good deal of time with his former cronies, and may even let his attention stray to one of his many old sweethearts. You must understand this and be patient, hard though it may be, for it is inherent in his nature to crave liking and popularity.

To hold his love, you must lavish love and affection on him. Go out with him a lot, get to know his friends and show a liking for them. Then give him all the solid comforts, so he'll see that in giving up his bachelor freedom he has really gotten something better in return—lay out his pipe and paper with his slippers, give him good food, make yourself always charming and attractive; and above all keep the home environment pleasant and peaceful. Have his friends in constantly for bridge, games, dinner, conversation. If you handle matters cleverly, his life will begin to revolve around the home. But relax your vigilance for a moment, and he will be more than apt to seek the gay, free life he knew before marriage.

Make no show of the jealousy he will frequently

excite in you. As a matter of fact, his little flirtations are usually quite harmless: he simply likes to reassure himself that he hasn't lost his touch. He tends to form a very strong affection for one person, and though marriage is no guarantee, its close association gives you the chance to make yourself that person. He is apt to marry on infatuation: it is your task to convert it into love. Loyal, deep down, he is not prone to seek divorce until conditions become unbearable.

He needs encouragement in his work, thrives on flattery, and must be made to feel that his talents are really superior to others. He loves children and pets, and should have at least two children. If you are clever enough to handle him properly, your life together will be enviably pleasant.

HAPPINESS IN MARRIAGE WITH A
CAPRICORN WOMAN

The worst mistake you can make with a Capricorn wife is to try to possess her utterly and completely.

Ruled by the planet Saturn, her nature is aloof, reserved, and conservative. She *must* be allowed to live her own life: going out alone or with others when she wishes, having her own car, bank account, and friends—in fact, living as much of a separate existence as is practical under one roof. If she indicates a preference for twin beds or separate rooms, that is not an indication of waning love, but simply an evidence of the craving for individuality inherent in her nature.

Not overly affectionate or sentimental, she will not demand constant attention from you. She is broad-minded: will permit you to live your own life with little questioning, and will expect the same consideration from you. Usually calm and philosophical, she can become on occasion (usually because of an invasion of her sacred privacy) very obstinate and difficult. Don't press for an explanation of this "mood"; wait until she volunteers it.

Once you understand her nature and the reasons why she acts as she does, you will find her wonderfully easy to get along with, enjoying a personal freedom greater than accorded by a wife of any other Sign. She is charming when she wishes to be: witty, and has powers of reasoning which go far beyond what men ordinarily expect of women. She does not like divorce, but if driven too far will resort to it without hesitation.

HAPPINESS IN MARRIAGE WITH A CAPRICORN MAN

Your Capricorn husband is at heart a philosopher and a poet, but the necessity for making a living has probably forced him to develop a business ability which is foreign to his inner nature.

Give him the beauty and depth of life he craves. Sympathize with his love for beautiful music and good books; create a peaceful and charming home environment. Respect his periods of thoughtfulness, for he needs to spend much time in silent reverie pondering over people and life: this satisfies the side of his nature which is frustrated in his daily business life.

Temperamentally, he is severe, determined and obstinate. His most trying periods will be during those cycles in which his ruling planet Saturn is afflicted, bringing him financial problems or distress. You must be more than ordinarily patient and understanding during these spells of depression: find little ways to please him, arrange trips and events of the sort you know he particularly enjoys, but which will not force him to exert himself to be sociable.

Meet his desire for privacy. Don't inflict relatives or your own friends on him when he is not in the mood; and if at all possible to avoid it, do not have relatives living with you. He enjoys working out his problems with you, but will resent even the well-intentioned interference of an outsider. Fortunately for you, the severity of his nature is tempered by patience.

He is practical and efficient once he has adjusted himself to the business world. He will probably demand that you account for every penny you spend, but this is an evidence of his efficiency, not of a penurious nature. He is usually a good provider, with the ability to make money.

He admires witty women, so keep yourself up with the world. Garrulity will annoy him: he prefers that you know when to talk and when to stay silent. In spite of his artificial wall of indifference and reserve, he can be very jealous: he likes the implied flattery of seeing other men admire you, but resents any show of your interest in them. Loyal and sincere, he stands much abuse. If there are children in the home, his interest will probably never stray from you. Only if denied affection is he at all apt to become engaged in a clandestine affair.

HAPPINESS IN MARRIAGE WITH AN AQUARIUS WOMAN

Your Aquarius wife is both ambitious and philosophical. That unusual combination of qualities holds both promise and menace.

By no stretch of the imagination is she a homebody; her hands were made for sapphires, not soapsuds. But if you accept her help and carefully arranged plans for your future welfare, she will have servants taking care of the soapsuds while she is free to enjoy social activities and make a comfortable home for you.

She dislikes poverty; abhors anything that is stingy or mean. She will actively resent anything petty in your nature, any inferiority complex or lack of ambition in you. She will be patient and coöperative during the years while you are climbing up the ladder, but if you fail through disregarding some of her advice, then expect trouble. Though having been in love with you for years, she may divorce you without hesitation: her philosophical mind reasons that if two persons cannot seem to work together toward the fulfillment of their destinies, they are better apart.

You must learn to confide in her your every thought and action, the bad with the good. She abhors anything secret or hidden. Trouble is certain if she hears of some transgression of yours first from an outsider. When you form the habit of taking her into your confidence constantly, you may be amazed at her breadth of mind and tolerance: she is inclined to forgive acts which would break up the average home if she is told about them frankly and given the chance to work out the problems logically from her own point of view.

Your Aquarius wife is, as you know, poised and magnetic. As a rule, she is very well liked by those who know her, disliked by people who meet her only casually. Her inner nature is actually spiritual and noble. Though apt to seem cold and aloof from life, she is really warm and given to great emotional reactions. When she loves you it is for all time, and she will leave you only as a result of some drastic force or disillusionment.

HAPPINESS IN MARRIAGE WITH AN AQUARIUS MAN

Your husband, if he has developed the full force of the Aquarius nature, has qualities of genius. That will not keep him from being human and making mistakes, but it may give you the patience you will need to cope with the twists of his character.

He is imaginative, intellectual, far-sighted, and creative. Driven by a deep inner urge, he wants to explore, experiment with, and test every emotion, situation, and person with whom he comes in contact. Let him. More than that, encourage him.

He finds it difficult to be practical about what he considers trivial matters of business and money. True, he likes the things money will buy and do, but he dislikes doing arduous or distasteful work to get it. He would much rather use his time in creating, or in promoting creative things.

You will have some hard decisions to make. He has a tendency to waste his time on projects which would ordinarily be unproductive, only to surprise the world by hitting on the one right thing which makes a fortune. The rulership of eccentric and erratic Uranus often creates inventive geniuses. (Edi-

156

son) . Your husband may cherish stubbornly a "wild" idea, only to carry it through to worldwide acclaim. (Lindbergh) . Through all his efforts will probably run an undercurrent of desire to help the masses, giving some great gift to humanity, or alleviating human suffering. (Lincoln) . He may make vicious mistakes, but will laugh them off and stand to his course regardless of scoffing and discouragement.

Many of his mistakes will seem unimportant to him, and he will never understand the fuss you make over them. At heart, he is still the boy who never grew up. He will have what he considers his little pranks, and when found out will be boyishly abject and humble, begging forgiveness and expecting it to be granted.

He may be unconventional and flirtatious at times, but you can best hold his love by being affectionate and self-effacing. Above all, learn his nature, and accept him as he is.

HAPPINESS IN MARRIAGE WITH A
PISCES WOMAN

This is one of the most sentimental and home-loving of all the Signs. Any disturbances in the home will probably be your own fault.

When abused, Pisces is hurt rather than resentful; to such an extent, in fact, that you may be disappointed in her lack of spirit. She is generally placid and calm, her infrequent outbursts of temperament taking the form of tears; you must go out of your way at such times to be patient and sympathetic.

Emotional, sensitive and idealistic, life to her is empty without love. She makes a wonderful wife, being unusually solicitous and anxious to please you in every possible way. Really she is like a child much of the time: simple, anxious to please, and self-effacing. Welcome her devotion, and show constantly that you appreciate her efforts. She will make few demands on you, asking at the most that you treat her with kindness. Friction in the house upsets her seriously, and any harshness or sharp word cuts right to her heart.

She enjoys mixing with people, and is never so happy as when she is the center of a gay little group in her own home. It is important to her to entertain a great deal. She likes friends, and generally has many people who are very fond of her. There is a danger in friendship for her, however, against which you must guard. Being very easily influenced, negative or vicious persons can implant ideas in her mind which will make her rebellious or discontented. Fortunately, this danger is active principally with persons who are vicious or who have ulterior motives, and against whom you can be on watch. But watch also well-intentioned but unthinking relatives.

NEW JOY IN MARRIAGE

Your Pisces wife actually *requires* that you be firm, decisive and dominating. She loves children, and finds her greatest happiness in caring for her own. Divorce is almost out of the question unless you yourself seek it, or unless she is pushed into such action by a dominating friend or relative.

HAPPINESS IN MARRIAGE WITH A PISCES MAN

His masculine traits modify the star-given nature of your Pisces husband to make him radically different from the women born under the same Sign.

He is much more firm and less patient. You will have to handle him carefully to keep down his explosive and volatile temperament. However, though quick to anger he is quick to forget.

He must be the leader in his home, resents having his orders questioned, and likes to have you lean on him for advice and guidance. You can expect him to be displeased if you try to hold a business position or carry on a career.

He is generally a capable money-maker, and with his ability at judicious saving and investment, is apt to build up a substantial fortune. He will actively dislike any inclination to extravagance in you. In fact, he is rather close in money matters, but you will probably be glad of that in later years when enjoying the financial independence which his carefulness may earn. He is very anxious to achieve financial security, and any efforts you make to help him will endear you to him forever.

You must be prepared to be absolutely honest and frank with him. Never do anything important without consulting him first. An attempt to trick him into anything is fatal.

See that he has all the home comforts. He will demand that you be a competent housekeeper. A home in the country or in a quiet suburb is best suited to his nature, since he is upset by noise and distractions.

By nature he is loyal and affectionate. You can best keep his love by harmonizing with the demands of his nature which I have mentioned, and by being always attentive, affectionate, and interested in his work and welfare. He generally likes one or two children: seldom more unless he feels he can always be sure of giving them the comforts and security of the good life. Divorce is apt to come only through your own negligence or wilfullness.

★ 6 ★

WILL YOU ATTRACT RICHES?

I CANNOT vaccinate you against poverty. Neither can I give you some magic formula for transmuting idleness into riches.

But I can do other things for you, things which are much more practical in this workaday, competitive world we live in. From the planetary influences under which you were born, I can tell you in what general field of endeavor lies your best chance of success, what type of investment is most favored for you, and what pitfalls await you both in your own temperament and in the deeds of others.

I have two ends in view. First, to set your feet on the lifepath of least resistance, for you will obviously progress fastest in the type of work to which you are temperamentally best fitted. Second, to permit you to combat the adverse portions of your destiny.

This last seems strange. But "the stars *impel*, they do not *compel*." The stars do point the path—but you alone are the master of your fate, and you may follow that path or not, as you choose. Once you know your probable destiny, you have the privilege of following its favorable signs, fighting against its pitfalls. If the stars give you a bent for invention, capitalize it—but if they balance the gift with a tendency to invest money unwisely, take that as a caution and govern your investment program with extra care.

The later chapter on Occupations will deal with specific jobs. Here I am concerned more with your search for financial independence in the broad sense, than as to whether you seek success in a profession, the arts, or in business.

ARIES

I wish I were opening this chapter with a Sign in which I could be less harsh. Please remember, however, that any severity rises from my conviction that honesty in regard to your future is more important than hurt vanity. As a matter of fact, you may already have noticed your particular handicaps and succeeded in submerging them.

Briefly, you have the ability to make a great deal of money. But unless you fight your nature, most of it will slip through your fingers. Your best chance for independence lies in the establishment of your own business, if you can only overcome your natural tendencies and save up the necessary capital.

WILL YOU ATTRACT RICHES?

Aries is the sign of power and lavishness. You enjoy a feeling of being superior, and an air of having inexhaustible funds. This may cause you to show off before others; you always like to reach for the check. Careless with money and extravagant, you develop a sense of order and business judgment only with supreme effort. You'll walk a mile to save carfare only to spend your last ten dollars on something you don't need. Money to you is something to be spent, and it burns a hole in your pocket or pocketbook until you have gotten rid of it—more often than not for something you don't really need.

The keynote to your whole character is impulsiveness. You are apt to rush into anything from a new business venture to buying a new piece of furniture with enthusiasm, regretting it later but never learning. You buy too quickly, you sign papers without proper investigation. Many an Aries subject has lost his lifelong struggle for riches by jumping headlong into an alluring proposition which he could have found was unsound or fraudulent. Your very anxiety to succeed in a hurry, and your impatience for quick riches is usually your downfall.

When an Aries subject does reach financial independence he usually gets there the slow way. Almost never will a get-rich-quick scheme work for you. Your safety lies in assuming that you will have to earn and save whatever money you will have in the future, dollar by dollar; and in setting about doing it systematically.

So learn to stop, think, consider. Then make haste slowly.

TAURUS

Taurus rules finances and monetary prospects. You therefore have an excellent chance of accumulating wealth. Furthermore, you will probably hold on to it. Most Taurians are good savers, and shrewd enough to keep their savings under their own control.

Your Sign is known as a fixed sign, and it seems wiser to attach yourself to some particular environment and grow with it or in it. However, your early life is apt to be a succession of changes until you find the right niche, at which time you have the capacity to settle down. This experimental phase is usually a good thing in that it guards against settling down in the wrong place; but it sometimes develops into a habit and the experimentation turns into waste motion, and a wasted life.

Your investments are generally lucky, provided they have two features: they should be conservative rather than speculative, and your money should stay close to your own control. Investments in unproved ideas, new inventions, and long-shot ventures are not for you—though the Taurian usually has to find that out for himself on at least one unfortunate experience. Your own business, or real estate which you supervise, is often your safest investment, since disaster lurks in placing Taurian money in the complete control of some other person. Your climb to fortune is usually slow but sure, and (unlike Aries subjects) that pace is in tune with your temperament.

Your dangerous period is between the ages of 22 and 30. Watch especially the dangerous Taurian physical appetites (particularly eating and drinking to excess, burning up your energies in night life, and forming unhealthy mental habits in relation to the love life), and get them under close control. Use these years to build up the desirable gifts of your destiny; training your excellent mind, making the right friends, and settling in the right occupational path. Deep in your character is a tendency for the Taurus mind to be vacillating and lacking in firmness, a weakness which submission to these strong physical appetites will bring to the surface.

The period between age 30 and 45 is generally marked with pronounced personal success for you. Your youthful mistakes are behind you; you have found your life work and become established in it, and you have become more solid in financial matters. You will now be feeling the urge to spread out, to grow, and this should be indulged subject to the two features of investment I mentioned above (conservatism and personal control). At this time, however, you should diversify your investments in two or more distinct fields, making certain that at least one is highly conservative.

The cycle between 45 and 50 will probably be your most productive. It is in that period that your biggest money should come and your financial independence be assured. If you have made mistakes, if you have lost money once or twice, you can count on this cycle of your life to recover the lost ground and put you back on the road to a competence.

GEMINI

The Gemini fortune (provided you overcome the duality of your Sign and accumulate one) is most apt to be created through the help of other people and their money. These persons are generally established before the public, socially prominent or politically powerful rather than men of business.

Your best chance lies in combining the power of your friendships with the persuasion of your words. Most successful Gemini persons are found before the public, where they can influence the thoughts and actions of other persons: they tend to change the mental mould of the public by using their powers of expression and ability to get others to do things for them, or to follow their lead. Patrick Henry, Brigham Young, Richard Wagner, Conan Doyle, and Walt Whitman are examples in their different fields.

Money seldom flows into your pockets in early life. This is the time when you should be developing your strong mind to its fullest, preparing it for what is to come. In these early years you are often dependent upon others for financial assistance, but you can generally win the confidence of those who possess wealth and position.

You are inclined to be shrewd in investment. In fact, you have a pretty dependable intuitive sense of what is or is not the right investment for you. Your fortune may be based on investment for the account of others, or on money borrowed from an influential person or from a bank. You often make money in mechanical industries (aviation, automotive, appliances, etc.), and you have the knack of making money beget money. More than any other sign, you tend to inherit legacies from near relatives.

Your danger cycle in financial matters comes between the ages of 35 and 40. At this time, even though well situated, you become impatient with what you consider slow progress and begin to scatter your forces and energies frantically in many directions. This rises from the duality of your nature, and if not controlled, may lead you to the loss of everything you have established.

CANCER

The late John D. Rockefeller is typical of this Sign. He was creative, conservative, and frugal; and those are your ruling characteristics in business affairs.

Your creativeness may suit you best for a career in one of the arts. But that quality is also very useful in business, for the creative faculty is essential in the planner, the promoter, the organizer, and the business pioneer. Your success will come through mental rather than physical work. You should make a good executive, with a particular aptitude for devising more efficient methods, creating advertising, and coördinating the work of subordinates. Usually you will do better as an employe than as a proprietor. Concentrate on *ideas*.

Your conservatism is a good quality, as is your frugality, provided you do not let them go too far. Coupled with your inclination to dream rather than do and your passivity, these qualities may lead you to sit back negatively and wait for opportunity, to refuse an opportunity because of a very slight risk.

Nevertheless, your stars blessed you with conservatism for an excellent reason. Highly speculative investments are especially dangerous for you. You aren't the type to get rich over night. Though you can make money in stocks, especially (strange as it seems) in substantial oil and mining concerns, you must follow those inner promptings, and investigate carefully beforehand. You are generally fortunate in attracting persons who can give you good advice on investments. And remember, pioneering in new fields though your work may be, your investments are best in established, safe things.

Do not envy what seems the more rapid progress of others while you are between the ages of 25 and 30. You are by nature aloof, reluctant to mix with life, more slow to learn business details and technique than some others. The period between 30 and 40 is apt to be your most productive, and by the end of it you should be well on the road to independence. Security means much to your type: plenty of insurance will remove the fear of uncertainty as to the future of your family and give you the peace of mind which you must have to work well.

LEO

The powerful Sun being your ruler, you are more gifted than most of the Signs, and your personal fortunes can soar to the skies. Leo is also one of the luckiest Signs.

Your greatest business asset is your ability to mix with people socially and make friends. You pride yourself on the wide circle of your acquaintance, and though you seldom actually plan to "use" your friends, nevertheless your greatest single step in life generally comes through the influence of some powerful friend. It is natural enough, therefore, that most Leo fortunes are built in positions where you must contact the public and win its confidence, using directly or indirectly your power of leadership.

Fortunately, you implement this bent for leadership with unusually strong mental qualities. This combination has been responsible for the public careers of such Leo persons as Joseph Pulitzer, Frank Munsey and Charles A. Dana (all of whom exercised their leadership through the public prints), Premier Mussolini, Napoleon Bonaparte, and George Bernard Shaw. These men have influenced the lives and minds of countless millions, and are typical of the Leo destiny.

Your worst pitfall lies beyond your personal control. There are periods, connected with afflictions to the Sun, when you are subject to financial reverses or may initiate ill-starred investments and financial ventures. In your particular case I suggest you accept the guidance of a day-to-day personal horoscope prepared by some reliable Astrological scientist.

Your carefulness with money will probably be misunderstood by others. You are not stingy or penurious; in fact, you like the best of everything and consider money as something to be enjoyed, spending it cheerfully when you feel you are getting value in return. You do, however, know the value of money and how to handle it; you are careful to make every penny do its proper job. When this carefulness of yours is misunderstood, as it often will be, do not let the attitude of others change your ways.

Leo subjects tend to create fortunes in early life. It is during this period that their minds are overflowing with inspirational ideas and they have the courage and outlook to blaze new trails. Your cycles of success are strangely regular, following a pattern of about three years. This cyclic turning generally gives you more than one chance to accumulate a fortune.

VIRGO

Virgo is the practical, commercial sign. It is ruled by the mental planet Mercury, however, so that you are constantly building, planning, changing, evolving.

In fact, the nervous, energetic radiations of Mercury can either build your fortune or tear it down. You have so many ideas that it is often difficult for you to decide which to carry out first. Too often you try to carry out several at once, with bad results. You have a serious tendency to rush into some new project with great enthusiasm, only to be disillusioned later on: whereupon you rush into some new and greener field to try your talents. Unfortunately, you are given to wishful thinking, a tendency to see only the favorable aspects of a proposition, minimizing or overlooking its disadvantages. You must learn to follow through, to concentrate, and to avoid waste motion.

You will probably be most valuable in some old, well-established firm where you can evolve new methods for creating business, or where you can plan or create advertising, publications, or new methods of presenting goods to the public. In such a concern your enthusiasm will automatically be balanced and concentrated into useful channels. You are fluent, and should be able to sway others in their business conduct.

You are able to make a good deal of money in your lifetime. How much of it you keep depends upon how well you control that enthusiasm and wishful thinking—also your leaning toward taking the long shot at big money rather than the slow way. You are fair prey for dishonest and misguided persons who have plausible propositions for doubling your money overnight. Force yourself, against your nature, to delve into the unfavorable aspects of propositions which come to you: try to balance your nature by looking on the black side. Instead of looking first at the possibilities for profit, look into the chances of loss.

WILL YOU ATTRACT RICHES?

A minor pitfall is your inclination to spend money on things you do not really need, necessary as you may tell yourself they are at the moment. Virgo women like to surround themselves with trinkets, jewelry, finery; men, with superfluous office equipment and over-elaborate tools of their trade. You also waste time and money through your liking for completely changing your environment every once in so often. (Just as a suggestion, try minor changes in the environment you have, until the urge passes.)

One indicated source of loss to Virgo persons, as inferred above, lies in the signing of legal papers without thorough investigation. You have a tendency to become involved in law suits and actions for breach of contract. Avoid, or at least secure competent legal advice on, any contracts of a technical or evasive nature. Your Sign also shows probable involvement with members of your family: positively, this may be a legacy; negatively, some complication which drains your pocketbook.

Your chance of making money is excellent, and you should be able to follow any of the professions or the arts with great success. But guard that enthusiasm, and try to keep enough of what money you make to defy your destiny and reach a position of financial independence.

LIBRA

This beauty-loving Sign needs the comforts and luxuries which money alone can supply. It is therefore true that money, second only to romance, is the most important thing in the world to you—though you would be the last to believe it.

Your pitfalls are much the same as those for Virgo. But where Virgo is too enthusiastic, you are impractical. Virgo is fooled mostly by himself: you are fooled by others as well.

This impracticality makes you fair game for unscrupulous persons posing as friends, and you must be especially cautious lest they take advantage of you in financial matters or induce you to speculate unwisely. (You are seldom victimized by strangers.) Your snap judgment cannot be depended upon. Money will come to you through persistent saving, bit by bit: by cautious investment in conservative real estate, proved inventions, listed stocks and annuities. You are quite apt to make quite a large sum of money through some especially timely investment. But watch your tendency to spend unwisely on expensive jewelry and furniture.

You are going to be happiest (and progress best) if your occupation is connected in some way with beautiful things, or in the pursuit of beauty. You will find that you have to force yourself to think of commercial things. An idealist, mixing with the commercial people of life does not please you too much. You can make money by applying these talents for creating beauty, and this should most definitely be considered when choosing your life work. A brilliant education is most often helpful to the attainment of success for Libra persons.

You must learn to scrutinize every expenditure carefully. Ask whether you can afford it; then whether the expenditure is really necessary. Save persistently, getting reliable advice in your investments and sticking to the safe and sound. If your life work harmonizes with your nature and if you guard against your impracticality, you should be able to accumulate a substantial fortune in your lifetime.

SCORPIO

This energetic Sign sets up financial security as the major goal of life. The Scorpio qualities of forcefulness and determination make it quite probable that this goal will be attained.

Your greatest danger, as far as accumulation of money is concerned, is your tendency to put on a "front." "Nothing but the best," is your maxim. You like to keep a little ahead of your neighbors in the outward signs of prosperity, and to travel in social circles always a little higher than you can afford. You must have the newest and best car, have clothes and jewelry which obviously cost money: you will take a taxicab home from a dance even if it means you must go without lunch the next day, and it is a major humiliation if a friend sees you riding in a street car or saving money in any other way. A windfall of money means a big party, which lasts until the windfall is gone.

The Scorpio mind is keen and productive of brilliant money-making ideas. If you end up without financial security it will probably be because you have wasted your substance in these showy, expensive habits of living, ruined by your own mistakes.

Another thing. Your Sign represents the secret forces of the world, and there is a tendency to persons born in this Sign to enter shady and unscrupulous business ventures. Scorpio breeds a good many fake stock salesmen, slick promoters, even embezzlers. This inclination to lavishness, over-expansion and lack of rigid scruple shows in certain ways in the case of Samuel Insull. Pathetically enough, Scorpios who go wrong could usually have made large honest fortunes had they concentrated their qualities in positive directions.

Most successful Scorpio subjects will make their money through promoting, rather than through working with their hands. They are good idea men, good executives and managers. Your best chance for success is in a line of work (acting or music, as well as business) where you can capitalize on your personality and creative faculty.

If you control your inclinations to lavishness, confining your promotional abilities to honest ventures, you should achieve financial independence. If you fail in one field, your exceptional adaptability permits you to change to another with the greatest of ease, so that it is not uncommon to find you changing your occupation three or four times in a period of a few years. This is not a harmful thing as a rule, for the promotional type is necessarily concerned with the new thing.

SAGITTARIUS

Your business ability is your best asset. True, many musical figures are Sagittarians (as witness Grace Moore, Beethoven, Deanna Durbin), but a study of their lives shows that the strong practical side of their natures entered largely into their successes. A sound training in business affairs, and personal development along commercial lines, will pay you.

The security which comes with financial independence means more to you than the money itself, for you have a very strong tendency to worry. Unless you have some element of security in your life, this

177

worry will hurt your work and hinder your progress. You must be extra cautious about assuming obligations which can burden you mentally: avoid buying too much on installments, and don't enter upon a purchase until you see your way clear to paying for it without strain. Resist pressure by those near to you to make unwise purchases. It is better in the long run for you to do without certain things than to feel insecure as a result of assuming obligations which worry and burden you.

It is unusually important for you to keep in mind this necessity for mental peace, for you have the inclination to spend even to the point of sacrifice for vanity's sake. Sagittarian women especially like perfect grooming and expensive dress, particularly expensive accessories. Satisfy that busy conscience of yours *before* you buy, rather than afterward.

You are a good manager or financial adviser for other persons. You can see ways of making money and investing it well when others are in doubt. Oddly enough you are not as capable when managing your own financial affairs, and should seek reliable advice.

Your best investment is often in your own business, or in one similar to it, for this Sign favors expansion. Try to keep some of your funds, however, in liquid form where they can quickly be turned into cash without sacrifice. I suggest this because emergencies are especially apt to arise in your life, usually connected with illness or injury to near relatives, which require cash. Your fortune should have been accumulated before the age of 45.

CAPRICORN

More than any other Sign in the Zodiac, you have to work for what you get.

You are quiet and unostentatious; you hate to push yourself, and you see persons with less ability getting ahead of you on bluff and glibness. You have a good business head, but your associates are slow to appreciate your talents. By working along quietly and doing your best, you will eventually attract favorable notice, especially for your dependability, but a little more push would do you no harm, foreign though it may be to your nature. Even so, patience must be the key word to your future, for you will tend to chafe at the delays which fate interposes in your life path.

You should be willing to spend much time training yourself for your occupation and should decide upon your life work only after great inner searching, for you must be especially reluctant to make changes as you go along. You may well work with the hands, provided that work is supplementary to mental work which precedes it. For example, the many famous illustrators, artists, musicians, designers, and skilled technicians born under Capricorn capitalize the delicate mental balance which the manual portion of their work requires.

Your work must be something which appeals to your imagination, or which requires mental application. It may be in association with others in some sort of public corporation: a university, hospital, or other public service. The professions and the creative arts are highly favored for Capricorn, though you must be satisfied to take the long time required to gain public attention to your work.

Most of the money you make will be made the hard way. Saturn, your ruling planet, goes through afflicted cycles which produce discouraging delays, obstructions and disappointments. Projects which turn out to be difficult for you should often be abandoned because of this.

Your money, hard earned, should be carefully conserved and conservatively invested. Gambling, or speculative investments, are unlucky for you. The best investment is in a practical business offering a staple product or service. Your own business can do well, and so can a partnership with a person who supplies the driving qualities you lack. Anything which takes several years to mature is generally a favored field of investment for you; examples being trust funds, government bonds and annuities.

Many Capricorn subjects lose their money after

age 50. As a matter of fact, your greatest danger cycle is during middle life and old age. The greatest care should be taken at this time to conserve what money you have accumulated. I wish that I could be more encouraging, but I would be doing you no service in concealing the facts. Forewarned is forearmed, and only by knowing the negative forces in your destiny can you combat and possibly defeat them.

AQUARIUS

This is the most inventive Sign in the Zodiac, and one of the luckiest financially. Not that Aquarians are immune from bad luck—in fact, their infrequent bad cycles last an exceptionally long time—but generally speaking, your ventures are favored.

Your mind, influenced by your ruling planet Uranus, is brilliantly creative, in the inventive sense. It dares to pioneer in realms where more stolid thinkers never penetrate. You can win the confidence of others easily, and your success lies in capitalizing on this faculty to carry out the amazing plans and ideas you have within yourself.

The mental, not the menial, occupation is best for you. You are apt to find yourself at the helm of new projects, doing the original thinking, giving orders rather than carrying them out. Your sign favors changing from place to place, and you will probably make your money in several different organizations or locations; always the new thing. You should be more successful in the large metropolitan centers than in small cities or villages.

Your realm is that of ideas. You may do well traveling, representing manufacturing concerns with new products. The amazing inventive genius of Aquarius is represented by Thomas Edison's pioneering mind; its flair for the adventurous by Lindbergh. Aquarians are by nature trail-blazers, innovators of new and progressive ideas which ultimately help the whole human race.

Your philosophical and mystical qualities often endow you with an intuitive sense about money matters. This may save you a large sum of money at some future time. Always consult this inner voice of yours before taking important steps in investments or business changes. Tend to trust your first impressions, for they are the unrecognized expressions of this intuitive guidance. Your "hunches" are pretty dependable.

Your pitfall is your possible lack of aggressiveness. You tend to be idealistic and passive. This lack of drive is usually not serious, however: though if it should be pronounced in you individually, you ought to force yourself to take action and capitalize your gifts.

Your destiny is quite well taken care of by the

ruling Uranus, and your chances for being able to retire early in life are good. Even after your financial independence is assured, however, you should let the creative side of your mind continue to function, though you may turn its powers to human service rather than personal profit.

You will probably never amass a large fortune. If you are a true Pisces, you do not want one. You do want security, but your demands are reasonable.

In Pisces we have the higher, the intellectual and spiritual, side of man. Your beautiful and mysterious ruling planet Neptune gives you power to do much good in the world. You generally do best by building on these higher attributes, taking your place as a leader in religious movements, educational circles and the arts. The careers of Pope Pius XI, Bishop John Vincent and many others demonstrate the high ideals and noble aspirations of which Pisces subjects are capable.

You are probably not very capable about handling money. You have a good business sense, but you are not equipped to battle in the fierce competition of the commercial world. If you do go into business, rigorous business training is vital if you are to keep from floundering about for years before finding your niche. The best place for you is generally in some confidential position where you work behind the scenes, using your intelligence to direct and manage others. Your desire for independence makes a small business of your own desirable, provided you can combat your destiny and defend yourself in competition: you may also buy a part interest in a business (especially in association with a person who supplies the aggressiveness you lack) and use your powers to build it up in size.

Though I will discuss specific occupations more in detail in a later chapter, I should mention here that many Pisces find their places in teaching, especially in dealing with very small children, because of their great capacity to mould youthful minds. There is also an inclination to go into radio, pictures, and the stage; also into the technical side of the creative fields.

Your greatest danger in financial matters is that others, especially close relatives and intimate friends, will impose on your generosity and take advantage of you. They may do this unwittingly, without evil intent, but in any case you may become impoverished. Your best advice will come from persons who are not too close to you; you should secure experienced outside advice before taking important steps in financial transactions or investments. Real estate, by the way (especially income property) is generally your most favored investment.

Pisces is a Sign which grows slowly, and only with much effort. You must never try to rush your plans through prematurely. Be sure of every step before you take it. Stay in one location or pursuit rather than shifting your interests from place to place.

You dream of a secure old age. You dread becoming dependent upon others, and you would rather die than become a public charge. Your feelings in this regard are so very marked that you should carry accident and health insurance, invest for safety rather than high return, and always keep some money ahead for the rainy day which comes to all Signs of the Zodiac, the favored as well as the less fortunate.

★ 7 ★

YOUR CHILD AND ITS FUTURE

NATURE is just. No Sign is absolutely good or bad. For each bad trait the planets bestow a good one, and though the Signs differ radically, each child has an equal start in life.

A Sign does become good or bad, however, upon exposure to the other forces which enter into the shaping of character and destiny: namely, environment, education and heredity.

The greatest of these is heredity. In these pages I hope to tell you how the tremendous force of heredity can be utilized to *combine* with the planetary emanations rather than oppose them, to the end that your child shall live the good life to which he is entitled.

As a simple example, suppose you have a weakness for gambling. If your child is born in Capricorn, his star-given characteristic of financial conservatism will offset this weakness which you have passed on to him. But suppose your child is born in Scorpio, which in itself produces the reckless, gambling type! Then he will have piled trait on trait, adding the planetary tendency to his inherited inclination. The resulting weakness will be well nigh irresistible.

Suppose on the other hand, you have a strong musical talent. Your child, born in Sagittarius, adds to the talent inherited from you his planetary leaning to music and creativeness. Now the piling of trait on trait produces a musical or creative talent of at least double power, and may even grant your child the birthright of musical genius.

You must study your child's character with extraordinary care. Learn your own weaknesses and talents. Learn those of your mate. Study the planetary character which the Sun imprinted on your child at the moment of birth. Then put your knowledge together, and suddenly you will view your child in a flood of new light. Armed with this new knowledge, the task of moulding your child assumes a new definiteness of purpose. You now know in what traits lie his pitfalls, and can combat them. More important, you know in what talents lie his opportunities, and can guide and develop them to full stature.

Who knows—perhaps you have presented him with a heritage priceless beyond any fortune of money!

Study the signs of the parents and child also to find the way to a more harmonious home life. Obviously, you will get along with the child better when you know *why* he acts as he does. A certain trait in him may irritate you to distraction. Learn what basic element in his character produces that trait, then either be patient in the light of your new understanding, or provide a new outlet.

Let's suppose he lies to you, apparently for pure pleasure. Study his character. Perhaps the objectionable trait springs from his star-given abnormally active imagination, which is a form of creativeness. If that is so, then persuade him to write little stories, buy him a drawing set and help him use it, start him on music lessons—any one of a score of things to turn that creativeness into constructive channels. Your little "liar" thus guided might develop into a great writer of fiction, for the two characters are closely allied.

Study the Signs and inherited characteristics also to shape your child's education, and to guide him into his life work. How tragically many fathers, glowing with pride upon the advent of a first son, have forced the child into a profession or pursuit for which the youngster was completely unsuited by nature. And how easily it could have been prevented!

Your child deserves enlightened guidance from the moment of his birth. Whatever thought, study, patience, and sympathy you pour out on his development is well worth while. It is the purpose of this chapter to point out the major pitfalls and possibilities in character development, weaknesses and talents, adolescent problems, health indications and the like, for children born in each of the 12 Signs.

But use these pages as a helpful guide, not as an Astrological Bible. Never forget, that, indelible though his star-given character may be, much depends on the influences which you and your mate, and even your parents before you, passed on to the child. His mind and character were moulded to a large extent at the time of conception, by heredity. Your traits of character, your ways of living, your physical constitutions—these are all recognized hereditary forces which the honest Astrologer does not dismiss, but considers as being inevitable and logical modifications of the known laws of planetary influence.

The foregoing remarks have been addressed to parents-in-fact. You who at this moment are planning to have children are blessed with a priceless privilege. You do not have to make the best of what already exists. You can plan your child's character and future by determining in advance what planetary character shall be bestowed upon him! This chapter, plus the earnest study of your own characters and Signs, will give you the basic facts upon which your plans can be based. Frankly, however, the subject deserves more discussion than space allows in this book, and it is my hope in the near future to offer you the advice you need in detail.

In the following detailed sections, the sexes are treated together. The pronoun "he" is used simply for the sake of convenience and therefore applies, unless specific exception is made, to both boys and girls.

For more detailed suggestions as to the life work for which his stars best suit your child, refer to his Sign in the later chapter, "Your Place in the World of Business."

YOUR ARIES CHILD

Whether boy or girl, your Aries child requires exceptionally careful handling and patient understanding.

He is apt to be headstrong, given to sudden fits of temper, and stubborn when you try to force him. However, he is tractable when treated with kindness, and intelligent enough so that he doesn't need to be told things twice. He must be persuaded and urged, reasoned with rather than forced. An attempt to "beat sense into him" will simply make him deceptive, secretive, unapproachable, and generally negative in personality development. Give him clear, direct answers to his questions, avoid cloudy, mysterious "explanations"; and never put him off with a "mind your own business" or "you can't understand that till you're older."

In educating your Aries child, keep in mind the fact that his mind is restless, and that his hands must be kept busy. He learns best by doing, and you should show him how to do things which will interest him. Round him out by emphasizing the practical, for he is by nature fanciful and a day-dreamer. He needs a normal background, mixing with other children preferably in a public school where he will have to learn to stand on his own feet and fight his own battles.

Without constant training, he will develop traits of laziness. Give him little tasks to do: make them regular, and try to build them into a sort of game. Pay him something for his work, and teach him habits of saving; he is not naturally thrifty, but early training can largely overcome his tendency to handle money carelessly in later life.

Do not encourage his frequent temperamental outbursts. The Aries child is too highly emotional for his own good. However, since his childish problems are very real and important to him, handle them with due attention, patience and tact. Instead of harshly demanding that he repress his temper, take a little time and explain how he only hurts himself (in the eyes of others) by being mean, petty, selfish or cruel. The same procedure applies to his liking for showing off, which can so easily degenerate later on into conceit and other disagreeable qualities.

As to his health, he is inclined to the normal childhood diseases, but especially those ailments having to do with the head, eyes, ears, and nose. Have his tonsils and adenoids checked regularly by a doctor. Use extra care about exposing the head and face to accident. His special hazards lie in overeating, carelessness in vehicles, stairs and dark places, and in foolhardiness. He has too little sense of fear for his own protection.

The period of adolescence will be very trying and dangerous. Tell him the frank truth (in a casual manner, without emphasis) about the facts of life and the reproductive functions of the body, for he or she will suffer permanent harm if this information first comes in a distorted version from schoolmates. Your daughter should be thoroughly warned about the cyclical phases in advance, so that when her body goes through its natural changes she will treat the event calmly and without alarm.

The training for Aries life work should begin quite early, possibly at 10 or 12 years of age, and the general foundation laid during the high school years. (You need decide only the general line of work— whether commercial, artistic or professional—for the same broad foundation will support any of the detailed occupations in each general group.) Whatever line you choose, however, it's wise to give him a substantial business training as well: he is too inclined, without such training, to scatter his energies and never become well grounded in business matters.

YOUR CHILD AND ITS FUTURE

Almost every Aries child should be exposed to accounting, typing, mathematics, composition, rhetoric and music.

YOUR TAURUS CHILD

Your Taurus child, as you know, is tenacious and determined. Don't try to stamp those qualities out of him: irritating as they are in childhood, they will be priceless to him in later life.

Try rather to turn that tenacity into constructive channels. You can't break his spirit anyway, for it's too strong: the only result of thoughtless punishment will be to estrange him and earn his hatred. When he flies into a temper (he is quite emotional and temperamental) let him severely alone until he calms down. When you must discipline him, tell him why, do it with no show of emotion on your part, and never humiliate him by referring to it later. He is unusually capable, industrious, and adaptable: you can easily invent some outlet for that determination and tenacity of his.

He will take to education quickly, and will enjoy excelling in his studies and being considered bright by his teachers and fellow-pupils. Just one caution: he is prone to develop an inferiority complex if disciplined or ridiculed in front of his classmates. When you find such a thing happening, consult with the teacher and find a better way of correcting his faults. His teachers must understand, as you do, that he cannot be driven, and that he must be allowed to think things out for himself.

Your Taurus child is sturdy, and not inclined to serious illness. Stocky and heavy set, his growing body needs an unusual amount of bone-building foods, curbing his avid appetite for sweets and starchy things. Whatever injuries he suffers will come from his tendency to carelessness. More physical than mental, he likes to work with his hands, and should be encouraged in tasks and games which will develop his body and provide an outlet for his overabundant vital energy. Taurus being an earth Sign, he will enjoy gardening and building: should be allowed a pet or two, for which he is given full responsibility.

The period of adolescence is not especially trying for Taurus children. However, their natures are experimental, and they are apt to know nature's secrets without being instructed by their parents. With this danger in mind, start early instilling in your child a healthy mental attitude toward sex—perhaps impart the facts of life earlier than you would to a less experimental child—and thus ward off wayward emotional habits and practices. His emotional life awakens early. Try your best to create in him the habit of confiding in you fully and frankly.

YOUR CHILD AND ITS FUTURE

YOUR GEMINI CHILD

Having absorbed the dual vibrations from his ruling planet Mercury, your Gemini child is complex in personality, hard to understand and manage. Make allowances for this duality when he does something completely illogical and unexpected. You must handle him with considerable firmness. His duality leads him to be angelic one moment, impish the next: you must gently mould him and try to make him hew to one line. Music lessons may help give him the faculty of concentration he so badly needs to acquire.

He is extraordinarily imitative. For that reason, select his playmates carefully and discourage those who are rude, ungrammatical, surly, or over-boisterous. Never make any promises which you are not prepared to fulfill—nor, for that matter, any threats—for he will tend, by imitation, to build up your example into what may become actual dishonesty in later life. Naturally, you will keep your own conduct, habits of thought and speech and so on, in channels which you want him to imitate.

You will probably find him overly sensitive, given to easy tears and pouting. Don't give him his own way too easily, and never give in to him under pressure of tears or sulkiness. This applies especially if he is an only child. He can easily develop your indulgence into adult habits of vicious extravagance. Teach him the value of money very early. Teach him also respect for the property and possessions of others, for he is naturally destructive. His most troublesome age will be between the ages of 6 and 12 years. Even at this period, however, do not punish him too severely: since he is intelligent and understands the psychology of punishment, physical severity is not necessary.

Gemini rules the arms and lungs, and your child's greatest susceptibility to illness lies in colds and lung disturbances. He must always be careful to avoid burns and bruises. Ruled by the mental planet Mercury, he has a tendency to nervousness which can lead to health disturbances. Overcome this by calmness and poise in yourself, and by a peaceful, unhurried atmosphere in the home.

In education, encourage a son in the use of words, for which he has an unusual ability. Induce in him, quite early, the habit of writing: perhaps in letters to relatives, plays for his playmates to stage and so on. Your daughter should be trained in work where she can use both her hands and brains.

YOUR CANCER CHILD

Your Cancer child is sweet, sensitive, and kind. He responds easily to affection, and enjoys the companionship of his parents, brothers and sisters.

The danger is that he will be handicapped permanently if his sensitive and retiring nature is not understood and properly moulded. Being perhaps too shy, modest, and negative, he should be encouraged in asserting himself to a greater degree, and made conscious of his personality as an individual. He is extremely apt to develop an inferiority complex. Naturally prone to suffer from self-consciousness, he should be encouraged in appearing before others in plays, concerts, and the like: generally built up in his ego until he considers himself the equal of the people he meets.

The emotional mechanism of Cancer, being ruled by the sensitive and changeable Moon, inclines your child to procrastinate, vacillate, and retire from life. Left to himself, he will not like to mix with the world. Only by encouraging him to play with other children on their own terms, keeping him in pretty constant social activity, will you overcome his tendency to live in a shell away from reality.

He is apt to be creative, evincing early an interest in music or art. Shape his education to give him free access to the beautiful things of life, and mould his appreciation of artistic accomplishment. Quite early, he can be taught to create objects of beauty for himself, even if in the beginning it involves simply cutting out paper dolls, or coloring and painting with crayons and water colors. As the only caution, however, keep this tendency within bounds, and do not let his pre-occupation with artistic pursuits keep him shut away from the vitally necessary human contacts.

There are no especial hazards to health in Cancer. This Sign rules the stomach, however, and your child should be taught to respect his digestion and treat it with consideration. Inclined to nervousness, he should not be forced to eat when emotionally upset: his parents should make it a point never to scold him or quarrel with each other at meal times. Take special precautions with cuts and bruises, because of the danger of infection to children born in the water triplicity, which rules the blood.

Remember your child's sensitiveness especially during adolescence. At this time, he or she may develop a sex complex which will permanently impair the full enjoyment of a normal life. The facts of life should be imparted quite early, while the Cancer child is too young to be easily shocked. Under no circumstances delay so long that the child learns these facts from other children, as that can do irreparable harm to his delicately balanced sensibilities.

YOUR LEO CHILD

Your Leo child is easy to manage and to understand. He loves his parents, and is fond of his home;

you can mould him readily with love, patience, and sympathy.

Don't confuse this with flattery, however, for adulation and his consequent feeling of importance will cause his natural charm to degenerate into vanity and boastfulness: the Leo child can easily become "too big for his boots." But harsh treatment or continual sharpness on your part will make him sullen, given to brooding on his sad fate.

Teach him the principles of democracy, and encourage him in mixing with other children on equal terms. He is too apt to think himself better than other children and act accordingly. He is acutely conscious of his environment, clothes, your appearance and your position in the community: he needs to learn early that the worth of people is measured by their qualities, not their possessions.

He is so very imitative that you will have to guard with special care your own deportment, grammar, personal habits, and so on. He will tend to become in great measure what you now are. Don't let him be too much with older people.

Leo being ruled by the powerful Sun, your child should possess a strong constitution and tremendous vitality. Leo governs the heart, and his future health hazards are mostly confined to cardiac disease. With this in mind, caution him against habits of strain, overwork, and nervous exhaustion. Teach him to relax, and don't let him overdo in athletics. Unfortunately, his unusual store of vitality leads him to be too active and strenuous for his own good, but his susceptibility to other diseases is less than normal.

Give plenty of time and thought to the matter of his education. He is exceptionally clever and intelligent, with strong executive and creative talents. If, as is probable, you decide on a practical training for him, see that he is also given a chance to develop his artistic and creative side. He may use this, perhaps to your surprise, to make his living: but even if he never commercializes it, this side of his nature needs an outlet to give full play to his strong nature.

Leo children being extremely emotional should be handled most carefully during adolescence, to prevent the development of complexes which can impair the future sex life. Perfect frankness is wisest. But impart the facts in installments, with extraordinary precautions against heavy emphasis: try to manage a casual, matter-of-fact air.

YOUR VIRGO CHILD

The stimulating and active rays of the mental planet Mercury dominated the Heavens at your child's birth, and imprinted on his brain a pattern which holds great promise. Being adaptable, he can be moulded to fit almost any course in life, but he is of such pliable mental material that you must exercise far more than ordinary care to see that the correct ingredients are instilled into his youthful mind.

Emphasize the practical in his training and education. Being somewhat inclined to the idealistic and romantic, he will be apt to retain his trusting innocence about people and life until he is well along into his adulthood. It is your difficult duty to dispell some of his illusions, to show him the reality of life as it is lived, at a fairly early age. Otherwise, the delayed shattering of these illusions will mean a brutally rude and bitter awakening: an awakening which, coming as it does in the wake of some wrong or betrayal, can warp his sunny, trusting nature into bitter cynicism.

He may be too bashful and shy for his own good, and you must throw him into the stream of life. By nature he is more introvert than extrovert, given to live too much within himself: you must subtly train and encourage him in expressing himself and adopting a more aggressive habit of mind.

Don't give him too much of his own way, for he can too easily develop traits of mental cruelty as a result. Overindulgence will bring out his latent inclinations to criticize, disobey, and oppose, making him mischievous and hard to manage to a dangerous degree. Give him physical as well as mental tasks to keep him occupied. Don't permit him to play too long or too hard, and never let work go over into the stage of drudgery for him. And above all, remember the necessity of developing a social consciousness in him; encouraging him to mix with children of his own age until he gets used to the idea of taking his place in the social world. Too much association with adults makes Virgo precocious.

As to health, Virgo rules the bowels. Your youngster is especially susceptible to colds, infections of the blood stream, and infections of the stomach and bowels. Watch his diet carefully, force him to take sufficient exercise (he will not do this without encouragement) and encourage him to spend much time in the outdoors.

YOUR LIBRA CHILD

Your child born under the beneficent rays of the planet Venus, in the air sign of Libra, is quite easy to manage. He is keen and intelligent, with an unusually well-balanced brain. Being sensitive, impressionable, and coöperative, he will not get into as much harmful mischief as other children.

In some cases this goes too far: nice for you, but not so good for the child. He is apt to be overly studious, spending too much of his time indoors reading. Not too sturdy of build as a rule, he actually needs encouragement in the rough outdoor life which in most other children must be curbed.

His mind will be capable of assimilating instruction at an early age. He will enjoy creating, and should be allowed to make simple things out of wood and cardboard. In school he will particularly need mathematical training, to prepare him for the complex and involved thinking of modern life which would otherwise be uncomfortable to him later on. Being adaptable, he can take up almost any line of work, and a complete general education is therefore desirable. He has the capacity to profit by a college course.

As to health, the primary caution is to keep him from overtaxing his mind and body. Being more subject than others to youthful illness, vaccination against the common communicable diseases is wise. This Sign rules the loins and kidneys, and he must be especially careful of injuries and disturbances in these regions. Though never bursting with health and vitality, he should, however, live a normally healthy life.

Libra's adolescent problems need not alarm you, for these children are intelligent enough to assimilate sane counsel. This mental development may give them the appearance of maturing at unusually early ages. Girls reflect the rulership of Venus by showing an early interest in boys; this interest is normal, and by sympathetic and watchful handling you can see that it is concentrated in channels of healthy friendship. Libra boys, however, have a tendency to take on slightly wayward habits (which sometimes is transmuted into a desire to leave home at an early age, or even to run away). The most effective discouragement of this inclination is a happy, frank, sympathetic and pleasant atmosphere in the home.

YOUR SCORPIO CHILD

The vitality and aggressiveness absorbed by your child from the ruling planet Mars fit him well for life's battles.

His strong will is exhibited in childhood in the form of tenaciousness which may make him unmanageable. He is headstrong, dislikes to take orders, and is given to fits of temper: mischievous, he will get into trouble with your neighbors. All these qualities, if permitted to develop negatively, will develop into a reckless disregard of the rights of others, and even cruelty. Positively, they almost assure his success in later life.

Handle him firmly, because he has a healthy respect for confident and constituted authority. Teach him to control his temper, and when you feel it necessary to punish him, do so without excitement or show of emotion on your part. Keep on the watch for evidences of obstinate, selfish, or overbearing traits, and combat them. Divert his forcefulness into constructive channels by giving him plenty of physical work and opportunity for exercise.

As for health; unless handicapped by heredity he has a strong constitution. Though, like all children regardless of Sign, he is not immune to the normal childhood diseases, the chance of really serious illness is slight. This Sign rules the generative organs, and in later life he may develop physical weaknesses in the reproductive system.

It is especially important that your Scorpio child be given a healthy sex outlook, due to the rulership mentioned just above. He should be taught bodily cleanliness, and an eye kept on him to see that no unhealthy sex habits are formed: Scorpio if not granted a normal view of sex matters early in life is apt to indulge in excess activity and sink to low levels of expression later on. This strong sexual force can be transmuted to a spiritual and mental plane however, a factor which accounts for the creative success of many persons in this Sign.

In education, bear in mind that your child is generally gifted for work which requires keen mental perception coupled with calm and orderly habits of mind. The sciences gives him good mental training, by capitalizing and developing his capacity for sustained thought.

YOU AND THE STARS

Your Sagittarius child is inclined to be a bit too aggressive for his own good. You will find it necessary to curb him when he becomes, as he often will, disobedient and unruly.

Your pitfall lies in the fact that he is also sensitive and intelligent. He will respond to kindness, and it will usually be better to admonish him firmly and reasonably rather than inflicting harsh physical punishment. Since he has latent leanings toward dishonesty and shiftiness, put a special emphasis in your training on honesty and truthfulness.

You will find him inclined to moodiness and spells of depression. Keep the home life as harmonious as possible, and never make the mistake of treating his childhood problems with any attitude other than serious respect. Give him games and mental pursuits to occupy his attention, and quietly see to it that he is seldom idle.

Sagittarius is a fairly healthy Sign. His greatest point of susceptibility is the head, and especially the ears: since this Sign also rules the thighs, he must be careful of injuries to those members. His sensitive mind seems to be reflected in a sensitiveness of body, but with proper attention to normal exercise and diet (especially calcium and protein, with plenty of fresh fruits and vegetables, which your doctor will suggest) he can be strong and healthy, growing up into normal adulthood.

His education should be, at least to some extent, along business lines, since he has a star-given business aptitude. His studies should be of the practical variety, things for which he can see some practical use. If he studies languages, for example, he will do better in the "live" group than with Latin and Greek. Encourage his natural interest in history, literature, and the sciences. Though he (more especially "she") is more apt to show creative talent, most probably in music, the practical side of his education should not be neglected. He is more apt to conduct a music school, for example, than to become a performing musician, and his business background will stand him in good stead.

YOUR CAPRICORN CHILD

It is going to be very hard indeed to get "close" to your Capricorn child. He will not naturally confide in you (or in anyone else, for that matter), and you will often be made to feel more like a stranger than a parent. This situation is delicate, and unless competently handled, may lead to a serious warping of his adult personality.

Perhaps the best method is for you to confide in *him*. Make him feel that he is a participant in your personal and family affairs. While you will never change or dominate him, yet you may arouse a feeling of reciprocity which brings you closer together.

He is serious in his outlook and manner, quiet, and apt to be moody. He generally prefers to be alone, and is reluctant to enter upon competitive sports with other children. Studious and intelligent, he is more mature than his years. Try to arouse him and encourage him in taking a more active part in social life—the word "social" being used in the broad sense of simply mixing with other people.

Let him know quite early that life is a tough proposition. Saturn being his ruler, nothing is going to come easy to him. An indulgent, sheltered childhood will let him in for bitter disillusionment later in life when the reverses come: he is apt to feel at that time that he has been tricked, becoming in consequence a moody, frustrated, resentful and cynical individual. Make your Capricorn child work for what he gets, put responsibilities on his small shoulders, teach him the value of money, and let him see the pitfalls of life which lie ahead. This should be done casually and cheerfully, but it must be done.

Saturn and its afflictions again enter into the matter of health. Extra care must be used to prevent accidents, especially those which occur in connection with vehicles, and through knives, guns and other dangerous weapons. Guard him also against

contagious diseases, with special care if there is tuberculosis in his heredity or environment: fortify him
with plenty of outdoor air and exercise, proper diet,
and check him quite frequently with a medical examination. With due care, however, he is sturdy and
no more susceptible than most other youngsters to
the childhood diseases.

Education is not much of a problem with Capricorn. Your child naturally takes to studies rapidly,
and your problem, if one arises, will probably be to
keep him from overdoing. Your daughter should be
given an occupational training, since she is more
than apt to prefer a career to marriage, or to continue to work after she marries. Give your son access
to the sciences, and let him develop his inventive and
inquisitive traits.

YOUR AQUARIUS CHILD

As I have remarked elsewhere in this book, the
Hall of Fame enshrines more Aquarians than any
other Sign. You may have a budding world figure in
your home.

But in his childhood, your primary duty is to overcome his natural passivity. He tends to sit back—he's
naturally rather retiring, anyway—and wait for life's
rewards to come to him without effort. You must
revise his outlook, and teach him to expect to work

for what he gets. Don't indulge him, don't give him rewards he hasn't earned; keep impressing on his plastic mind that life is real and earnest.

His education should major in experimental subjects, those in which he becomes accustomed to using those strong mental powers of his. Chemistry, physics, biology, philosophy, psychology—all give him a chance to do original thinking. Outside of this emphasis, his education should proceed along normal lines. Encourage this studious and experimental bent outside of school by furnishing him with tools and mechanical sets; materials for his radio, chemical, photographic, and other hobbies. Don't discourage him on an original line of thought, even though you know it's a blind alley: let him follow through for himself.

Adolescent problems should not exist to much of any extent for this intelligent and normal Sign. Give your Aquarius son or daughter a patient and frank explanation of the life forces, careful never to give an impression of hiding anything. When their curiosity is appeased in a normal manner they accept the bodily functions as a matter of course. Their emotions can be expected to mature early.

In matters of health, considerable caution is required. The mechanism of brain and body is highly intense and nervous in Aquarius. Diet must be rigidly controlled, with an emphasis, subject to medical advice, on nerve-building vitamins. There is susceptibility to lung and stomach disturbances, and extremely cold climates are inadvisable. Since Aquarius rules the legs and ankles, caution should be instilled at an early age to guard against accident to these members. However, in spite of the tendency to delicate and slender build, the child is more than apt to be physically strong and tenacious.

YOUR PISCES CHILD

Your Pisces child can be handled best by winning his confidence and trust.

He has a pleasant personality, is apt to be attractive, and mixes easily with other children. He is by nature honest and truthful; you must see that these qualities are recognized and rewarded; never accuse him of lying until you are certain of your facts. His mind is highly tuned, and he is sensitive and responsive. Thriving on affection, he is happiest in a home environment where sympathy and attention abound: friction between his parents will seriously distress and worry him. Try subtly to build up his self-confidence and aggressiveness, because he has none too much of these necessary qualities in his inner nature.

You will probably find him subject to quite a few minor health disturbances in his early years. Give him a well balanced diet to build up resistance to his tendency to colds. In view of his inclination to dropsical ailments later in life, discourage his appetite for sweets. Train him against all excess in eating and drinking. His principal accident hazard is to the feet.

He has a strong artistic bent. He also enjoys fabricating things, and his education should include opportunities to develop this. Prior to school, give him an outlet for this desire by supplying him with the materials for painting, building, sewing, and so on. Your son should be encouraged in his liking for making things and tinkering, your daughter in helping about the house. A general education is best, and public schools are much to be preferred over private schools or tutors.

If you have built up mutual trust and confidence, you will not have much difficulty with him or her during adolescence. However, the facts of life should not be imparted too early, due to the Pisces tendency to introspection. Best wait until the child either asks a definite question or the subject comes up naturally. Then give only whatever information he wants at a time, saving the rest until a later opportunity. Needless to say, such conversations should be open, frank, and casual, avoiding any atmosphere of "importance" or mystery.

★ 8 ★

YOUR PLACE IN THE WORLD OF BUSINESS

I READ in a so-called Horoscope recently that the person was ordained by the stars to be a dentist. How completely ridiculous that is! Astrology was a settled science long before the ancients could have known of dentistry or any other modern occupation.

What the stars *have* done is imprint upon you a certain definite set of characteristics and aptitudes. Suppose you are blessed with that unusual combination, deft hands and a good brain? Then you are perhaps fitted to be a dentist—but fitted just as well to be a watchmaker, a radio technician, or even a portrait-painter if you happen to add to your equipment the creative faculty. A given set of characteristics may fit you equally well for any one of several occupations.

Moreover, these fundamental characteristics in your star-given birthright may take on outward evidences which seem at first glance to differ quite radically. The writer of fiction doesn't seem to have much in common with the accountant—but if the accountant's talent happens to be in laying out new systems of record-keeping, then both persons are evidencing exactly the same basic faculty, that of creativeness.

The radiations of your planets, aided or opposed by your heredity, gave you certain abilities. These abilities find their best outlets, and hence give you your surest chance of success, in the occupations which I will name under each sign. If you have not yet selected a life work, this advice will point out your path of least resistance and greatest opportunity. If on the other hand, you are already settled in your job and feel it unwise to make a change, then read between the lines of my advice and figure out for yourself how you can remould your particular job to more fully express and utilize your star-given abilities.

Suppose you are an automobile mechanic, and I say that your character has fitted you to be a writer. You will know that your latent writing ability implies the possession of creativeness. Then apply that creativeness *in your present job* to better yourself— develop some of the many ideas which come to you into actual inventions, any one of which may make your fortune, or create new and better systems for handling the work in the shop, thus demonstrating to your employer that you are fitted for bigger things—and so on without end.

Most of us do not choose our life work, but rather fall into it by accident. Perhaps our parents decided it for us, perhaps a friend or relative made a place into which we slipped without real thought, perhaps— and most likely of all—we took the first job which came to hand and stayed in that line of business ever since because of the risk of changing.

I do not tell you to change your work, even though you may find in these pages that it is not suitable for your particular talents. I do tell you, however, to use my advice to improve yourself within your present job, building on it to perhaps higher things than you would have thought possible.

Nowadays hardly any occupations are restricted solely to men or to women. Therefore I am not sepa- rating the sexes in the following sections, but will leave it to your discretion to make the separations yourself. Also, as you notice, many occupations are suitable in general for any one of several Signs: so analyze the occupation in the light of your Sign's particular set of abilities, and decide in what branch of that occupation you should specialize. And finally, as it goes without saying, your educational and envi- ronmental equipment must play a large part in your choice.

NATURAL OCCUPATIONS FOR ARIES

Your Sign rules the intellectual faculties, and you are also fitted for contacting the public. Your tendency to domination and willingness to assume responsibility makes the executive type of position best for you: your creativeness equips you to do the thinking, planning and organizing which is part of the executive's job. (A person who gives orders to others but who does not *plan* for them is simply a foreman, not an executive.) The following fields are natural to you:

HEALTH SERVICE: including nursing, hospital superintendent, doctor's attendant, X-ray technician, laboratory worker. You use here your efficiency, poise and cool head; sympathetic without being sentimental.

TEACHING: and educational work in general. You have a good mind for details, patience, and the ability to handle children.

SECRETARIAL WORK: your mind is quick and alert, qualified to move ahead if such a position proves to be a stepping stone to larger responsibilities.

ARTIST, INTERIOR DECORATOR, DESIGNER: these lines bring forth your creativeness, originality, freedom from conventional restraints, and they call on your business acumen as well. You harmonize with artistic people.

DRAMATIC AND MUSICAL PROFESSIONS: good, you combine emotional potentiality with perseverance, and are an extrovert. Musically, your best instruments are harp, piano, violin and cello.

MEDICAL: Mars rules surgery, and in character you are capable and industrious, quick but calm. Specializing in eyes, ears, nose and throat should be successful, and there is a probability of your obtaining a politico-medical position.

LAW: best in corporation or criminal branches, with an aptitude at politics. You make a good trial lawyer, being fluent and alert.

CONSTRUCTION: as an independent builder, contractor or architect. Your originality permits designing new-type plans and finding cost-saving shortcuts; your aggressiveness enables you to set up in your own business.

SELLING: your aggressiveness and extroverted nature, plus your good mind, fit you for selling; better at selling ideas and projects than actual articles.

ACCOUNTING: you will weary of the details of an actual bookkeeping position, but it may lead to an executive position with an accounting flavour, such as banking, insurance home-office, and brokerage.

RADIO AND AVIATION: you are adaptable and original, with no fear of the "new thing." Positions with a technical aspect are best; also in the same

general field, motion-picture sound man or technician.

You are best fitted for work which requires a combination of manual and mental facility. Not particularly creative, you are more a follower than an
originator, though an individual horoscope might
contradict this in some cases. You have versatility
and adaptability, but prefer routine work to tasks
which require frequent mental re-focussing. You are
steady, deliberate and patient, and can therefore
choose an occupation where you may need years to
work up to the top. Don't let your restless (and
vacillating) mind lead you to change positions too
often.

OFFICE WORK: clerk, secretary, switchboard operator—good for girls who plan to marry early and
would therefore waste a lengthy or expensive occupational training; also for men as a stepping stone
to jobs higher up the ladder.

NURSING: you enjoy helping others and don't mind
the physical side of the work—better in a hospital
than with a private doctor; being fearless, controlled,
and liking travel, you make a good airline stewardess.

TEACHING: a bit limited, best at mathematics,
languages, or English literature; more suited to high
school and college than grammar school work.

YOUR PLACE IN WORLD OF BUSINESS

THE ARTS: acting, music, dancing, painting, writing— Taurus is frequently successful here, but more as an exponent or reporter than a creator, best at developing ideas created by others.

MECHANICAL: carpenter, plumber, engineer— your hands are deft and you can stand the hard physical labor at the beginning of your career; your uncanny ability to forge to the front probably forecasts your own shop, business, or engineering practice.

PROFESSIONS: in the medical field, you are especially adapted to public health work—in the legal, to prosecuting attorney, judge, or other politico-legal position. Your confidence-inspiring personality also fits you for brokerage, especially in real-estate, investments, and insurance.

NATURAL OCCUPATIONS FOR GEMINI

Your duality of mind, provided you can force yourself to learn concentration, gifts you with versatility, ability to fill a position which requires several different talents. With your nervous temperament, a creative type of work is best. A position or occupation which makes use of your fluency with words is excellent; also one which capitalizes your ability to coördinate your hands and brain.

THE ARTS: you have a natural feeling for music

219

and rhythm, and for form. The creative end is best for you—original writing (especially dramatic writing for stage, pictures and radio), painting, drawing or designing, and character acting; in music you will do best as a composer.

OFFICE WORK: best where you are called on to meet the public, capitalizing on your personality, as a cashier or salesman—also as a secretary, court reporter or other position which utilizes your speed, accuracy and efficiency without being monotonous work.

CONSTRUCTION: you're original, are able to visualize a thing before it is constructed, can put your ideas on paper for others, and have a good eye for detail—architect, builder; also industrial designer or inventor, model maker or dress designer.

SALES WORK: your good personality and mercurial temperament, plus your knack of winning confidence, stand you in good stead here—you can sell the "one-call" sort of product or service.

PROFESSIONS: think twice before deciding, because your temperament may balk at the long grind of educational preparation. In medicine, specialize in chest and throat; in law, domestic relations and corporation law. You should do well in politics also.

YOUR PLACE IN WORLD OF BUSINESS

NATURAL OCCUPATIONS FOR CANCER

The combination of conservatism and creativeness in your birthright fits you for the planning functions in business: your frugality and ability to handle money makes it possible for you to succeed in setting up and managing an enterprise of your own. You also have unusual powers of analysis, and an instinctive discrimination as to what people will like.

OFFICE WORK: pleasant personality and conversational ability fit you for positions which contact the public, such as receptionist, information clerk, telephone operator, correspondent. Cancer women are not sufficiently aggressive for retail sales positions except in lines such as perfumes and jewelry, where your love of beauty and delicacy makes up for this lack.

NURSING: practical nursing only, since your inclination to early marriage makes a long training impractical. Your love of children opens up GOVERNESS work, and your personality and patience makes you a good COMPANION to an elderly person.

THE ARTS: you have definite talent. As an actor, the rulership of the Moon makes you imaginative and emotional; temperamental in the useful sense. As a writer, you possess good plot sense— Cancer men may utilize their flair for judging public opinion in newspaper work. Your good eye for form and color equips you for designing and art.

FINANCIAL: your ability to analyze and judge values, plus your conservatism and confidence-inspiring personality fits you for banking, investments, insurance, and real estate. You can sell ideas, which opens up the position of account-executive in advertising. In these fields, try to get the opportunity to use your talent for organizing, and for managing the affairs of others.

THE PROFESSIONS: the law is good, especially if your work takes a political turn. In medicine, your best field is specializing in diseases of women and children.

OWN BUSINESS: trades favored are automotive, radio and electrical, oil, and ladies wear.

NATURAL OCCUPATIONS FOR LEO

This fortunate Sign has great mental and inspirational gifts, coupled with the power of leadership, and the ability to make friends. Take unusual care in choosing your occupation, because your tendency to change several times during your life may mean wasted years.

OWN BUSINESS: favored lines are florists, foods (especially bakeries and confectionery concerns), millinery, decorating.

YOUR PLACE IN WORLD OF BUSINESS

SALES WORK: Leo women make excellent department store and specialty-shop saleswomen, especially in women's wear. Leo men sell ideas, projects, and large products better than small-unit items.

OFFICE WORK: not so good unless there is a chance for individual responsibility or off-pattern creative work. You don't follow orders any too well. Take the routine office job if it's the only thing open, but seek for the chance to step up, or to develop new ideas which will broaden your work.

THE PROFESSIONS: in medicine, specialize in obstetrics and womens' diseases, also heart ailments. In law, use your flair for making helpful friends. You have a natural bent for the diplomatic service; your firmness and air of authority fits you also for a commission in the Army or Navy. Your fluency, natural leadership, and anxiety to help humanity fits you for the church. Teaching is excellent.

THE ARTS: Leo rules the entertainment world, and you have much better than average possibilities in radio, stage, motion pictures, music and writing. Lecturing is also good; painting not quite so favored. Cultivate your artistic talents at least as a hobby, perhaps commercializing them when you have developed them sufficiently.

MECHANICAL: feature the creative rather than the manual end. Building, architecture, automotive, and electrical lines are best. Don't neglect your inventive ability, even though you carry it on as an avocation; you may hit on something that will make your fortune.

NATURAL OCCUPATIONS FOR VIRGO

Virgo has fluency, a knack for detail work, and too much creativeness for his own good. By the latter I mean you get such a flood of ideas that you try to carry out too many at once, and fail to take sufficient thought before going into a new enterprise or changing policies in your own business.

OWN BUSINESS: try to team with a partner or employee who will curb your enthusiasms and your tendency to let important things lie neglected while you fuss with absorbing details. Favored lines are all those requiring finance and accounting; also hotels, real estate, book stores, dress and beauty shops.

OFFICE WORK: an executive position definitely lies ahead; to start, you're best in accounting jobs where you must convert dry figures into significant facts—statistical work is especially good. Secretary, cashier, department store buyer, accountant also favored. Virgo women have more business ability than women of most other Signs.

TEACHING: fluency, retentive memory and good personality are your assets; best specialties, languages, music, and commercial subjects. You make a good librarian, and can fill executive positions in library work as well as teaching.

THE PROFESSIONS: try for the research type of work, where your creativeness and patience with detail is valuable. Law and Medicine are especially suitable for Virgo talents. Engineering is excellent, also its outgrowths of technical positions in radio, telephone, and mechanical lines.

THE ARTS: you're too practical to be a good actor or classical musician, as a rule. Writing is excellent, better in factual articles and reporting than fiction; you make a good editor, re-write man, or proofreader. Look for openings in the commercial side of the arts, as in publishing, radio station management, and so on. Good at lecturing and announcing.

SALES WORK: your personality permits you to get along in sales, but you seldom care for it; usually you use a sales position as a stepping stone to executive or inside work. You make a good sales-manager, if you can toughen your easy-going nature and make yourself more of a driver. Best sales lines; real estate, investments, automobiles.

NATURAL OCCUPATIONS FOR LIBRA

You have a strong love of the beautiful. Though more attracted to work of creative than commercial nature, you nevertheless possess a practical streak which helps you to make money out of creative or artistic pursuits. Your nature is finely balanced, which is helpful in certain occupations (such as research or purchasing), detrimental in others (as in selling, where you are too prone to see why the customer shouldn't buy your goods).

OWN BUSINESS: shipping, especially water-borne; importing and exporting, mining and metal processing, womens' wear, florist, beauty shop.

OFFICE WORK: not too good, except for something to do while waiting for marriage or a promotion. Best in one of the lines mentioned in the section just above.

THE ARTS: your ruling planet Venus is favorable to actors, musicians, and painters. Designing, decorating, millinery, landscape architecture, and other practical expressions of the artistic are good for you. In writing, your greatest opportunity lies in dramatic criticism or dramatic writing; your mind is creative, philosophical, and you are a good analyst of character, which make writing a logical field.

THE PROFESSIONS: your ability to weigh facts makes you an excellent judge—in legal practice, however, specialize in research, preparation of briefs, and arbitration, rather than actual trial work where your impartiality puts a drag on your pleading. You are willing to do painstaking work and possess the ability to profit by higher education; you make a good doctor or surgeon, chemist, clergyman, or scientist. Your liking for pure intellectual attainment makes a profession more desirable than one of the standard commercial pursuits.

NATURAL OCCUPATIONS FOR SCORPIO

You are probably slated for leadership. You have a dominant will and forceful personality, with plenty of initiative and aggressiveness. You have the single-mindedness which, unlike Libra, drives straight to your goal without thought of opposition. But choose an honest occupation, for your leaning to subtlety can easily lead you into the devious and shady path.

OWN BUSINESS: druggist, barber, metal working, machine shop, jewelry, warehousing.

OFFICE WORK: favored only for getting a start, so choose a job which has plenty of future. Avoid your inclination to get mixed up in office politics.

NURSING: excellent for Scorpio women, especially in lines where your force has an outlet, as a hospital superintendent, or where your natural magnetism can flow through your hands, as a masseur.

MECHANICAL: railroading, draughtsman, architect, aviation, all are favored; you have marked engineering ability, expressed in your methodical, deep-thinking mind.

THE ARTS: writing is especially favored, particularly the involved sort of construction required in the mystery story (which also employs your deviousness of mind) . Your best writing will be done in collaboration.

THE PROFESSIONS: your method, force, and unusual coördination of hand and mind make you an excellent surgeon or dentist. Your magnetism and fluency equip you for occupations requiring oratory, such as trial lawyer, minister, or political figure. The military professions are especially good. You have the capacity to absorb the long-drawn-out, rigid mental training required for most of the professions.

SALES WORK: excellent. You're persuasive, dynamic, compelling and fluent. See that you sell only ideas or products in which you have honest faith. Your executive position in business will probably have a selling flavour—you would be the logical person to merge several large concerns into a gigantic combine, for example.

NATURAL OCCUPATIONS FOR SAGITTARIUS

Business ability is natural to you. You are direct, and have a power of intuition which permits rapid and accurate decision. Your ruling planet Jupiter comes close to guaranteeing success, so see that whatever occupation you choose has an unlimited ceiling.

OWN BUSINESS: you have considerable organizing and directing ability. Your Sign favors textile dealing, foods, production and selling of literature, mimeographing and manuscript bureaus, shipping and other activities having to do with water.

POLITICAL: Jupiter favors statesmanship, and fits you for political positions, such as magistrate, assessor, elective office, and civil service appointments.

THE ARTS: choose the business side—if an artist, specialize in advertising and commercial art. In literature, you are best in the production and selling end; publisher, editor, or bookseller. Photography and museum employment are excellent for you.

THE PROFESSIONS: again, try for the business and commercial side. If a surgeon, the management of a clinic is better suited to you than private practice. However, your abilities of analysis and patient investigation, willingness to work and to rise slowly, plus your studious nature, supply you with an excellent character for professional work.

SALES WORK: only as a start. Best when you work on commission, and in a line where you have personal responsibility. Choose the sales job that leads to executive work; favored lines are department stores, insurance corporations, banking institutions and brokerage houses.

NATURAL OCCUPATIONS FOR CAPRICORN

You are the plodder; industrious, accurate; despite your consuming ambition (a product of your fear of poverty and insecurity) you have little of ostentation and "flash." Choose an occupation where persistence and plodding pays out. One unusual talent you possess, however, is your ability to drive a hard bargain.

CIVIL SERVICE: the security and automatic promotion will mean much to you (a factor which applies also to routine and office work with certain large corporations). Teaching, postal service, government accounting offices; all are good.

OWN BUSINESS: one where stability and reputation rather than flash is the essential. Manufacturing (staple products), wholesale clothing, mining, construction, agriculture (including nurseries especially), are favored; also dealing in real estate and managing the property of others, and hotel proprietorship. An association with a partner who supplies the qualities you lack can open up other fields, but you should govern the buying and financial ends of such a business.

YOUR PLACE IN WORLD OF BUSINESS

THE PROFESSIONS: excellent, in those fields where you do not have to build up a public practice. Biology, forestry are good; public health work and almost any branch of science. In the law, you make an excellent behind-the-scenes man; also very good as an investigator or detective.

THE ARTS: not so good (unless heredity has overcome your introverted personality) in branches requiring public appearance. Writing is excellent, however, especially of the sort which requires patient investigation and compilation of facts; you might make an outstanding historian, or write great historical novels; the research department of a motion picture studio would be ideal for you.

COMMERCIAL: keep your eye on the purchasing agent's job, for you will be able to perform his duties perhaps better than a subject of any other Sign. You have the patience and application to work up to it, so try to get a start in a position which leads in that direction.

NATURAL OCCUPATIONS FOR AQUARIUS

This Sign, less than any other, requires vocational guidance. You are apt to succeed at whatever you undertake, provided it has a "broad" aspect. You are driven by a consuming desire to benefit humanity in the mass, to do good, and your occupation must give that desire an outlet. Your mind is logical, inventive and constructive.

OWN BUSINESS: paradoxically, in view of the above, going into business for yourself is not usually advisable. Unless heredity has given it to you, you lack shrewdness and the desire to make money solely for yourself. Your best business is one which involves beauty (clothing, designing, and so on) or one which you can feel is of benefit to humanity over and above the profit you make from it.

THE PROFESSIONS: favored, especially medical and nursing. Teaching, social work are excellent. The law is favored, though it will be as a rule a stepping stone to some position of public service. The occult holds opportunity for you; Astrologer, Christian Science practitioner, mental healer, and so on; the church is ideal, especially in its evangelistic aspects. Exploration and scientific research are natural to you.

OFFICE WORK: favored only as a stepping stone to advancement. Seek the position, such as private secretary or executive's personal assistant, where your creative faculties can have some outlet. Force yourself to pay particular attention to detail, for you are by nature visionary and a trifle impractical, your eyes more on the big things ahead than on today's routine.

THE ARTS: excellent, in all branches. Public entertaining is especially favored for those born in the first nine days of this Sign; stage, radio, television, motion pictures, lecturing—all are good. Writing is natural, though your work will tend to be of the non-popular type and hence slow in attaining recognition; you will have to force yourself to be "commercial" in your choice of subjects and treatment.

MECHANICAL: not too good in the work-a-day branches. Build up your inventive faculty, however; your ideas may bring fortune, or at least improvements you suggest will result in promotion. You can go into sales work which requires a mechanical background.

SALES WORK: good. But always offer a product or service which you honestly feel is going to benefit the purchaser, for you cannot put any driving force behind a proposition in which you lack faith.

NATURAL OCCUPATIONS FOR PISCES

The best occupation for you is one in which advancement depends upon actual ability or seniority rather than "front" or forcefulness. You are naturally passive and lacking in self-confidence, willing to let others get ahead by walking over you.

OWN BUSINESS: dangerous, unless you have an associate who supplies the aggressiveness you lack. Choose such an associate with extraordinary care, because of your tendency to be overly trusting; and then force yourself to see that he carries his share of the load. Don't do any of the bargaining yourself unless heredity has supplied you with the hardness you naturally lack.

HUMANITARIAN: any occupation which ministers to the wants and suffering of others is good for you —nursing, teaching, welfare work, activity in political reform movements, and the like. Your psychic and intuitive powers fit you for the occult studies.

OFFICE WORK: excellent, with your patience and willingness to assume responsibility. You have a good mind for detail, and are especially suited to positions of confidence and trust such as confidential assistant, treasurer, and so on. Civil service is good, since advancement does not depend upon that "push" which you lack.

THE PROFESSIONS: excellent, especially those with humanitarian aspects such as medicine. Your patience with detail, coupled with your excellent mind, makes you a good engineer if you can overcome your difficulty in concentration. Inventive and creative work is favored, especially that with a mechanical flavour.

THE ARTS: good— Neptune, your ruling planet, favors the artistic and inspirational activities, though you will have to bolster up your self-confidence if you are to make a success in acting, music, or other fields which involve public appearance. Writing is excellent, especially that of the highly imaginative sort.

SALES WORK: not recommended, unless heredity has supplied you with unnatural aggressiveness and self-confidence. In any event, choose a line which involves your contacting the same customers over a long period of time, rather than the "one-call" product.

⋆ 9 ⋆

YOUR SOCIAL LIFE AND FRIENDS

"**I** WISH I knew her better." You've often said that.

"I've met him several times, but we just don't seem to click." You've said that even more often.

And, "What's wrong with me—why don't people like me?" Perhaps you've even said that, though strictly to yourself.

For all of us want popularity. We envy tremendously the person who always seems to be at ease, who without any apparent effort is the center of attention in any group. Some of us who lack the brilliance of wit and conversation, the sparkling good looks and magnetic personalities given to others and withheld from us, develop complexes and neuroses —and then proceed to act in a manner which simply makes matters even worse.

Actually, attracting friends and getting along socially with other people is not a magic power, but a faculty which can be developed. Perhaps the stars haven't blessed you with natural magnetism—but nature is just, and you have other qualities which the magnetic person lacks. Perhaps when these latent powers of your personality have been developed, the magnetic person will come to envy you: for though he may attract friends more quickly, you will probably hold them longer, and that after all is infinitely more important.

There are, of course, many things you should do to "win friends and influence people" in the bulk, regardless of their Sign or yours. I am not concerned with that here. I will tell you about the special qualities in friendship and social relations most prominent in each of the Signs. With this new insight into the hidden character of a new acquaintance— knowing his sensitiveness, his likes and dislikes, and so on—you will see what you must do to harmonize with his personality and win him for a friend. Upon studying your own Sign, you will see yourself as others see you, and learn of qualities which you should enhance or suppress; developing your attractive qualities and submerging those which might repel or displease other people.

You have seen elsewhere in this book the chart of Signs compatible and incompatible to you by nature. As I have said before, and will say again, there is no incompatibility you cannot overcome if you know from what hidden roots of character this natural opposition springs. You must put forth more effort to win a friend in an incompatible Sign, but that is all.

While in this chapter I am speaking primarily of friendship, much of the advice has a direct bearing on choosing business associates and harmonizing with them, and with courtship. Also, the pronoun "he" which I will use throughout for the sake of convenience and simplicity, refers to friends whether men or women. Finally, I am not going to insult your intelligence by supplying obvious conclusions: in other words, when I point out that "your such-and-such friend is touchy," I am depending upon your common sense to draw the logical inference of, "so don't step on his toes."

A faculty for friendship can greatly enrich your life. Don't simply sit back and wait for people to come to you. Don't let people pass from your life without effort, leaving your friendships up to the vagaries of chance. Do something about it. Work at friendship. I will give you here the raw materials, but you must fashion them yourself.

FRIENDSHIP WITH ARIES

Aries is a good mixer, and easy to meet.

He likes center stage, and prefers to monopolize any conversation. Flatter him, especially on the brilliance of his intellect, though not neglecting his looks and possessions: you can lay it on pretty heavily. Don't try, however, to impress him with a show of your own abilities, possessions, and accomplishments: he values sincerity and simplicity, and judges you more for what you are than what you try to appear to be. You must let him take the lead in practically everything, even at the risk of dimming your own personality.

He (though more especially "she") is pleased by little gifts and attentions. He will enjoy granting favors to you, and will be quick to help you when you need aid. Give him affection, sympathy, flattery, humor, tact and understanding, and you will find him a true and loyal friend. He is quick to anger, but quick to forget and forgive; don't take too seriously his exaggerations or the things he says when irritated: never carry through a quarrel to its end, but drop the argument quickly and keep out of his way until he has cooled down.

IF YOU ARE ARIES, force yourself to let others bask in the spotlight occasionally; give a little flattery in return for that which you get; keep your flaring temper under control and learn to apologize after it has burst its bounds; and once in a while give your friends the fun of winning an argument or making a decision.

FRIENDSHIP WITH TAURUS

Taurus, ruled by Venus, is naturally friendly and sociable, though his attitude on first meeting is apt to be critical, cool, and aloof.

He is suspicious of motives—yours and everyone else's—which makes obvious flattery unwise, though he appreciates honest admiration. Sincerity, truth, and directness work best with him. Though early in your acquaintance he seems inflexible and unyielding, the winning of his confidence will make him plastic to your will and personality. He seems dominating, but actually is not; this impression rises from his possessiveness and jealousy—resentful of your other friends, he likes to be the one to take the aggressive lead in your affairs.

His sense of humor is excellent, and your surest appeal to him is through it. He has an especial distaste for criticism of his personality, mannerisms, voice, possessions and friends. His tendency to scrutinize everyone through a mental microscope may occasionally make you uncomfortable. A bit ostentatious, he likes to show off his physical and mental prowess, but he enjoys sharing his possessions and entertaining. He will not want you to spend money on him, and you should hide any superiority over him in your financial or social position. At times stubborn and hard to get along with, the ascendancy of Venus will soon make him tractable and good company again.

He enjoys the country, and likes outdoor sports. Though he enjoys contact with good minds, he adapts himself pleasantly to simple conversation, especially delighting in the amusing and trivial things of everyday life. You will find him loyal in friendship, and quick to defend you against criticism. He dislikes fickleness, gossip and scandal. Any kindness you show him will be long remembered.

IF YOU ARE TAURUS, try to warm up more to new people. Cultivate more trust in others; check your tendency to show off; and recognize the fact that your friends are entitled to be friendly with others than yourself.

FRIENDSHIP WITH GEMINI

A Gemini friend is hard to win and harder to hold.

Highly popular socially, he is always the center of a crowd. If you manage to get him by himself, you find him reticent and hard to approach. His conversation will be impersonal, and his silence will make you feel self-conscious. Strangely enough, there are times when his volubility will sweep you off your feet, for his volatile ruler Mercury gives him a sharp intellect and an ability to use words well.

Make allowances for the duality of his Sign. He

will be friendly and unfriendly at the same time; like you immensely one moment and discard you the next. You will enjoy his companionship when you can understand him and accept his idiosyncrasies; but never expect too much from him.

Your best approach is through his intellect, so be posted on the latest books and plays, keep familiar with business and political developments—and have on hand a copious stock of gossip about outstanding personalities, and even about persons in your intimate circle. You will have to take a terrific interest in him and his affairs, but if he seems interested in yours, it's strictly simulated and the conversation will soon veer back to him. His restless mind flits from topic to topic in conversation. On first meeting, don't appear too serious or too glib, and don't talk in riddles or epigrams.

His mind is complex, with a deep undercurrent of involved emotional reactions. He seldom says outright what he means; more often he says one thing while his mind is thinking quite the opposite. Your Gemini friend will lead you an active life, but at least it won't be dull.

IF YOU ARE GEMINI, try to overcome your curse of duality; make up your mind, and say what you mean. Learn to affect an interest in your friends' affairs, and make an effort to be more warm and steadfast.

YOUR SOCIAL LIFE AND FRIENDS

FRIENDSHIP WITH CANCER

Cancer is hard to win in friendship, but easy to hold.

Never affable with strangers, his natural reserve and retiring nature erects seeming barriers, though they melt away upon closer acquaintance. Quiet and passive ordinarily, he can nevertheless rise to a situation which calls for volubility and determination. Don't talk too much about yourself until you're pretty sure of his interest in you: be willing to take weeks or months in your campaign.

He is highly discriminating, and your time will be wasted unless you are at least his equal in mentality and possessions, with similar business, social, and intellectual interests. Though not a snob, he is acutely conscious of social differences and is not inclined to mingle with those below him in the scale. He is proud of his accomplishments, background and possessions, and will appreciate your noticing and commenting favorably upon them.

If You Are Cancer, don't let your periods of deep thought give the impression that you are sullen or moody; make an effort to be sparkling and sociable, and to put new acquaintances at ease in your at-first-glance forbidding presence.

YOU AND THE STARS

FRIENDSHIP WITH LEO

Leo is sincerely democratic and enthusiastically sociable; genial and cordial even on first meeting.

You must, however, be content to play the satellite, dancing attention upon him. If you don't, someone else will, because Leo is always the center of the group, at his witty best when surrounded by admiring and applauding friends. In fact, it may not be easy to attract his attention to you personally, his time and energy being so fully occupied with the friends he now has.

Though he almost never suffers from any inferiority complex, he isn't overly conceited. The attention he draws without effort is simply a tribute to his aggressive and compelling nature. He is generous, often generous to a fault. He demands from you an unfailing cheerfulness and a constant show of affection. Take an interest in him, his work, and his other friends. He has an avid appetite for flattery, and will never suspect your motives in offering it: lavish flattery is the surest way to his friendship.

IF YOU ARE LEO, try to take more of an interest in the affairs of your friends, their hobbies and lives. Don't talk quite so much about yourself. See if you can't make a few real friends out of your many acquaintances.

YOUR SOCIAL LIFE AND FRIENDS

FRIENDSHIP WITH VIRGO

The winning of a Virgo friendship is a real feather in your cap.

He is surrounded by a wall of reserve, no matter how genial his surface manner may be. Unlike some of the other Signs, this wall is real, not just a protection for a retiring nature. He is complacent: he is satisfied with the friends he already has, and doesn't want any more. Too much interest on your part, or any obvious anxiety to win his friendship will make him suspicious of your motives.

But he has his vulnerable point. He likes the brilliant mind, the studious, intellectual, quick, progressive person. Needless to say, he will see through any sham or pretense to these qualities on your part: you must actually possess them. Even the occasional earthy Virgo must be approached from the intellectual side rather than the emotional. An alert personality, a fluency with words, and a flair for crisp humor will capture his attention.

Never, no matter how well you come to know him, pry into his private life. Don't be boisterous, don't flatter, don't urge him into a round of social activity. Be always sincere, conservative, and strictly honest with him. His friendship, once deserved and won, is everlasting. He will give more than he takes.

IF YOU ARE VIRGO, and (which is unlikely) wish

to attract more friends, let down your bars a little: be less touchy about remarks which others may make to you, and make yourself approach people instead of waiting for them to approach you. Incidentally, don't become involved in the lives of your friends, for it never turns out quite right. Your big favors, done without expectation of repayment, always seem to boomerang.

FRIENDSHIP WITH LIBRA

Libra, though easily attracted, does not make a deep or close friend.

He likes a great many people and counts them as friends, but he isn't inclined to cement his friendships by making sacrifices or giving much of his own time. He is apt to be impressed by your possessions and position in the community: he likes showy things, and will appreciate your lovely home and expensive car more than your sterling qualities of character. In justice, however, he is not so much mercenary as he is anxious to get ahead in the world, consequently prone to value your accomplishments in terms of your "show."

He himself is a good conversationalist, and admires wit, brilliance, and social flair in you. Invite him to parties at your home, introduce him to your more impressive friends, and lead him on a social whirl. Quite wordy and fond of hearing himself talk, he has a weakness for indulging in criticism, severity, and sarcasm. No matter how long your acquaintance, he is always weighing the evidence for and against you (the symbol of Libra is the Scales), and may turn against you very suddenly; though this reversal may be without apparent reason, he will be able to justify it in his own mind.

To win Libra for a friend, you must be mentally rather superior, or at least seem to be. He will actually be attracted by a certain amount of affectation and artificiality. Secrecy also intrigues him, and he is drawn to anyone who is aloof and seems surrounded with a cloak of mystery. Parade your high ambitions, and give Libra a lot of personal attention.

IF YOU ARE LIBRA, forgive my harshness in the foregoing remarks. You have probably already recognized and overcome your faults, but read this section over again just in case. In addition, make a greater effort to be considerate of others' feelings, and to be pleasant: praise people occasionally; and relax that dynamic personality of yours a bit, for your terrific mental activity keeps your friends under a tension too high for pleasant companionship.

FRIENDSHIP WITH SCORPIO

Scorpio acts like a friend rather than looks like one.

He's apt to be blunt and outspoken on first meeting. Not at all inviting in aspect, he is often misjudged as cold, calculating, and overbearing. Actually, Scorpio represents the mysterious and secretive forces of life, and never does the obvious thing. He will never swarm over you, but once past the slow process of winning his friendship, you can count on him in any crisis.

He is generous and kind, but in a practical way. Not given to idle talk or show of affection, he is a person of deeds rather than words. Effusive thanks will embarrass him. Take especial care not to offend him with slighting remarks, for he takes everything seriously. He admires fluency, and your best approach is through an ability to talk interestingly and expressively about topical things. He enjoys orderliness and neatness of dress, dislikes heartily any undue familiarity or boisterous treatment. Like Virgo, your forbidden gesture is the rough slap on the back. He likes sports and outdoor life. In spite of the impression given by his manner, he really relishes companionship, and enjoys sharing simple pleasures with his friends.

If You Are Scorpio, try to be more affable on

first meeting; learn to turn an occasional compliment; submerge that natural sternness and try to laugh more often; overcome your tendency to criticism and sarcasm, and make the effort to invite the confidences of others.

FRIENDSHIP WITH SAGITTARIUS

Fascinating Sagittarious demands more from you than light surface appeal.

He won't be easily impressed by your possessions and position. Instead, he will look for whatever sterling qualities are in your character, and ignore everything else. Your bearing must be conservative and poised: it will help if you show an honest interest in his work and friends. He is pretty dominating, and you will find it necessary to submerge yourself to a large extent, playing up to his interests rather than featuring yours.

He is much more mental than physical: enjoys music, art, literature, and the more erudite side of life in general. Your keen appreciation of beauty will mean more to him than any social activity you can offer. Generally serious, and never given to light laughter, yet he has a dependable sense of humor. Intelligent conversation is the best approach on first meeting. You will find that he admires accomplishment and will appreciate your high ambitions: this is not because of any mercenary attitude, but rises from his progressiveness and active dislike of mental laziness. Don't be insistent in involving him in your sports and pleasures, for he usually prefers a life confined to his family and a few intimates of years standing.

IF YOU ARE SAGITTARIUS, soften that austerity of yours on first meeting; be less blunt, and avoid talking overmuch about yourself, your reverses and illnesses; cultivate geniality, try to laugh more often, and overcome your tendency to lean on others.

FRIENDSHIP WITH CAPRICORN

Capricorn is attracted only for the moment by the flamboyant, volatile personality: he selects his permanent friends for the same qualities of dignity and reserve which he prizes in himself.

He is generally a solemn sort of person, even depressed: Saturn is his ruler, and this moody planet does not bestow gaiety or lightness. Appeal to him through his emotions, for he is very sentimental and sympathetic. Sympathize in your turn on his life, struggles and hardships—he usually has more than his share—and you will arouse his genuine fondness. Break through his somber outlook with a constant unobstrusive cheerfulness (never a boisterous spirit, however) .

YOUR SOCIAL LIFE AND FRIENDS

Though he will occasionally follow a stronger personality, he will never enjoy doing so: he wants to be the leader in friendship and set the tempo in his limited circle. He is jealous of his friends, and—a warning—is not above using them if he can do so gracefully; he cannot help being shrewd and calculating. Capricorn is an earth Sign, but in friendship it's really more like rock—reliable, solid and steady, but also uncomfortable, inflexible and unyielding. He's inclined to be selfish, and you will have to cater to that quality. Don't violate his secretiveness, for he will actively resent any attempt to penetrate the veil of mystery he draws over his life and thoughts.

IF YOU ARE CAPRICORN, set about exchanging some of your firmness for gentleness and forbearance; lighten up your outlook, and be on the alert for little ways in which you can help others; be more generous and friendly in spirit, give as well as receive, and learn to go halfway in meeting people, instead of expecting them to come all the way to you.

FRIENDSHIP WITH AQUARIUS

Aquarius is hard to meet, but easy to know.

Pleasant and agreeable by nature, he is usually shy and retiring, reluctant to meet new people. Peace loving, he relishes an atmosphere of harmony and quiet. Excitement and much social activity is distasteful to him. He cherishes a secret side of his nature which few are ever permitted to share, and you must not pry or snoop into his guarded privacy.

The best approach is to take up and enjoy his amusements, keep away from controversial subjects, take an interest in his work if he seems to invite it, and let him see that you are mentally alert. He will like to share your ideas if they are original and progressive. As a rule, he is interested in social problems, and it's fortunate if your mind also functions along philosophical lines. Loving music and literature, he is also creative, inventive, and frequently mechanically minded. He is usually an enthusiastic participant in outdoor sports, and incidentally, many Aquarians take up aviation as a hobby. Once won, he makes a strong and considerate friend.

IF YOU ARE AQUARIUS, see if you can't overcome some of your natural timidity; be less retiring, and share your thoughts with others; simulate, if you can't feel, an interest in the other fellow's interests; watch your tendency to verbosity, and catch yourself when you embark on one of those interminably dull technical discussions to which you are addicted; make yourself more practical and less visionary, and overlay that sensitiveness of yours with a layer of thick skin.

FRIENDSHIP WITH PISCES

Pisces is the most useful of friends.

He is very affable and magnetic; likable, he attracts and holds many friends. His nature radiates kindness and interest in everyone with whom he comes in contact. But more people like him than he likes in return, for one reason—his abnormal sensitiveness. So treat him with unfailing kindness. Never be brusque or harsh. Let him indulge his yearning to talk at length about his life and problems, to lean on you, to bring you his most trivial worries even though he bores you at times. Never turn him away without sympathy and help. Be prepared for the fact that he will expect to monopolize your time.

He is exceptionally fond of social activity, and likes to be the center of a little coterie of admiring friends. If people fail to cluster about him, he is deeply hurt. Since he wants to feel that people like him for himself alone rather than for what he may possess, give him (more properly "her") a lavish offering of compliments on his appearance, the impression he makes on others, his accomplishments, and so on. Never make the mistake of being overly forceful or insistent, especially in regard to something he does not particularly care to do. Ask favors with the confidence that he will actually enjoy granting them. He is generous, sincere and loyal: he will never desert you in time of crisis.

IF YOU ARE PISCES, try to dwell a little less on your own problems and troubles, because the other fellow has some of his own; don't be too talkative; let your friends live their own lives without too much regulation from you; cultivate calmness and poise when disturbing situations arise. Above all, get over that abnormal sensitiveness of yours and stop imagining slights and slurs where none exist. Everybody honestly likes you, so stop worrying and fretting about it.

YOUR BIRTHRIGHT OF HEALTH AND LONG LIFE

THERE is a story about a man who asked an Astrologer, "In what city will I die?"

The Astrologer asked him why he wanted to know.

"Because," the man is supposed to have answered, "then I would never go near that place."

I'm afraid that's rather too simple a recipe for an eternal life. Yet Astrology can come surprisingly close to giving you just such a recipe for a healthy one. It can tell you your star-given bodily weaknesses and the illnesses to which you are particularly subject, so that you need "never go near those places."

Of course, Astrology isn't the be-all and end-all of health matters. Your Sign might, for example, show no star-given susceptibility to tuberculosis. Nevertheless, if a tubercular weakness were passed on to you by your parents and forefathers (heredity), or if you were brought up without the proper food, sunlight and fresh air necessary to build a strong constitution (environment), then you could easily possess such a susceptibility. Again, Astrology is not a vaccination, and cannot protect you if you are exposed to contagious diseases.

Astrology does, however, help you immeasurably in two ways. First, each Sign rules certain organs or members of the body, and its subjects are susceptible to injury or illness relating to them. Second, and perhaps more important, many ailments and injuries rise directly from the traits of character which the planets imprinted upon you at birth.

The strong influence of Character upon health and length of life is expressed by most religious faiths, especially in the tenets of Christian Science, and is today admitted by the medical profession. Suppose a person is given to worry and nervousness—isn't a case of stomach ulcers a perfectly logical consequence? Or suppose he is terribly strenuous and prone to overexertion—who doubts that he will develop heart disease?

I will point out to you in these pages your weaknesses in matters of physical health, and your particular susceptibilities to accident. Guard against these special weaknesses just as I have told you to guard against weaknesses in character. When I said that you, for instance, were prone to bitter sarcasm, and suggested the cultivation of patience, I wanted to help you stop hurting others. Now when I say that your overly high tension leads to nervous exhaustion, and necessitates a smoother tempo of living, I want you to stop hurting *yourself*.

My advice will be deliberately couched in general terms. No Horoscope, no matter how carefully charted, can possibly take into account the effects which heredity and environment have had upon your star-given physique. So a suggestion of mine to watch your diet, for example, is meant as an instruction to go to your doctor and have him diagnose your ailment and prescribe for you specifically.

My whole accent is on *prevention* of illness, in the belief that the foreknowledge of a weakness will permit you to set about building up resistance to that weakness before trouble begins: to lock the barn door before the horse is stolen. Incidentally, I hope to see the day when people let their doctors prevent illness rather than simply cure it. Too many of us look upon the doctor as a sort of medical fireman, to be called in only after trouble is upon us. So learn here your tendencies to physical weakness; learn from your doctor whether those weaknesses actually exist in *you*, and then keep such tendencies under rigid control.

YOUR ARIES BODY

Aries rules the head and the head region, and this naturally inclines you to disorders having to do with the brain, as well as the eyes, nose, and ears. There is also a sympathetic rulership over the stomach and kidneys, with a consequent tendency to weakness in those organs.

Your character aggravates these weaknesses. Your aggressiveness and dynamic energy causes you to overdo, and to tax your strength beyond endurance, which brings on nervous exhaustion. Headaches, to which you are subject, should be regarded as symptoms of some related trouble. There is some inclination to appendicitis, also to rectal difficulties; Aries women are subject to disorders of the generative organs.

Fortunately, your forceful Sign has blessed you with a sturdy constitution. It is your duty to protect and cherish it. You can avoid many of the disturbances which afflict Aries by lightening your tension, perhaps even going to bed at the first indication of approaching illness. As to diseases in general, your resistance is high, though there is a possibility of apoplexy or paralysis in later life. Living at a normal pace, not only in connection with activities of the brain, but as to eating and drinking, is the keystone of longevity for you. Keep the tension low, and watch your diet.

My records indicate that broken bones are more common to Aries than to the subjects of any other Sign. You're always in a hurry; so cultivate caution, and be especially careful in connection with stairs and automobiles. Mars rules sharp instruments and explosives, which means that you have a special hazard from accidents involving knives, guns, blasting, fire, and the like; keep a guard on your natural carelessness when exposed to dangers of this sort.

YOUR TAURUS BODY

Taurus rules the throat and those organs located in the throat region, including the organs of speech, the thyroid and other glands, and so on. There is a logical tendency to tonsilitis, laryngitis, diphtheria, goiter, and similar ailments. Protect the throat region against weather and contagion, avoid abuses of it, and check with a doctor when an ailment appears in this part of the body.

Most of your health hazards arise from your character. Your strong physical appetites lead you to serious over-indulgence in food and drink. The natural consequences are obesity, heart ailments, apoplexy, alcoholism, and serious digestive disturbances. Sensible diet and moderation are your watchwords. Guard also your weakness for violent outbursts of temper, which if long continued bring on mental disorders, burst blood vessels, strokes, brain tumors, and high blood-pressure. Moderation and restraint again.

Your constitution is earthy and strong—it will

probably need to be. In early childhood Taurus may develop weaknesses in the chest region, sometimes influenza and pneumonia; in such cases, moderation and careful living is more than ever necessary in adult life. Your danger cycle is between ages 25 and 30, at which time you are most subject to over-living, over-work and over-strain. You have no special accident hazards.

YOUR GEMINI BODY

Gemini rules the lungs and the chest region, which inclines you to pulmonary pneumonia, tuberculosis, bronchial disturbances, and the like. You should take especial care of yourself in especially cold climates, and in changing weather or moving from one locality to another of radically different climate. Get plenty of outdoor exercise, and plenty of sleep— more of the latter than most people seem to need.

Anyone as versatile as you, as active mentally, and as excitable and supersensitive, is going to suffer from nerves, nervous disorders, and the organic ailments which result from over-tension and worry. Your neuritis and rheumatic pains in the joints and nerve centers will usually trace back to your character weaknesses. Try very hard to cultivate mental, nervous, and physical poise; force yourself not to worry and fret, and seek for a calm philosophy of living. The exercise, fresh air and sleep mentioned above, plus avoidance of excess in the physical appetites, will go far toward calming your overly high-strung nature.

Whatever your constitution at birth, it has probably been dissipated at least to some extent by your wastage of nervous energy. More than most people, you must reconcile yourself to healthy, normal habits of life. Any accident or injury will usually be the result of your inattention and lack of concentration.

YOUR CANCER BODY

There seems to be a widespread belief that natives of Cancer are susceptible to the disease of the same name. There is no connection; the names are alike only through meaningless coincidence. You have no special susceptibility to cancer.

Your Sign rules the stomach and the lower chest region. Your weaknesses lie in the direction of gastric disturbances, weak digestion, and asthma. Keep a check on the tonsils and adenoids, being careful also not to over-strain the vocal cords. Cancer, ruled by the Moon, also controls the fluids of the body, giving rise to possible trouble with the secretions of the glands, spleen, gall bladder, and so on. In women, this rulership brings susceptibility to acute disturbances in the vital organs and their functions, especially during gestation and childbirth. Take especial care to avoid over-strain during the menstrual period. In both sexes there is an inclination toward appendicitis.

Your physical weaknesses arising from character are the above, but carried to extremes. You worry far too much. Worry, for example, can take an ordinary gastric weakness and develop it into a full-fledged case of stomach ulcers. The old phrase, "worried sick," often applies quite literally to you. Very often the only medicine you need is to stop fretting about spilt milk, and about milk which you fear may be spilled if this-and-that comes to pass. As to length of life, the fact that both John D. Rockefeller and Mary Baker Eddy were Cancer should reassure you. Injuries are most apt to come to your legs and thighs. Take special precautions against blood poisoning whenever the skin is broken.

YOUR LEO BODY

Leo and the ruling Sun combined to give you a tremendously vital constitution. Leo rules the back, which makes it necessary for you to avoid physical strain in that region; but most important, it rules the arteries and the heart. Heart disease and ailments of the circulatory system are your primary health hazards.

In character, you will tend to develop these weaknesses rather than combat them. You go to extremes; bursting with energy and vital force, you scatter these priceless assets. This has especial reference to the sex life, for Leo dominates the seat of the emotions and leads you to excess emotionalism and over-activity in sex matters. Avoid also becoming addicted to tobacco or liquor, because too seldom can you keep these habits under control. Alcohol in particular holds serious physical dangers to you, for your mind is finely balanced and can be too easily thrown into mental disorder. Avoid also the overwork and over-strain to which you are prone, because both lead directly to aggravation of your heart weaknesses. Don't indulge either in bursts of temper or hard physical labor.

As I said, the stars have given you a constitution which will stand a lot of abuse. That is no reason for abusing it. A chain is no stronger than its weakest link, and your rule is therefore to live sensibly and avoid excess.

YOUR VIRGO BODY

Virgo is on the whole a very healthy Sign. Fortunately, you have few temptations to excess; I say fortunately because it happens that high living and heavy drinking are especially dangerous for you. Also, you are more reluctant than you should be to ask for medical advice and care; you try to keep going, hoping that you will throw off your illness, until sometimes it's too late for the simple treatment and quick cure which would have been available earlier. Paradoxically, many Virgos become hypochondriacs, dwelling on their ills and magnifying them.

Virgo rules the intestinal canal, the solar plexus, and to some extent the lungs. Your special weaknesses (though minor) are in disorders of the liver, spleen and pancreas; gall stones and peritonitis; with some inclination to intestinal poisoning and appendicitis. Your digestion may be none too good, which makes it wise for you to avoid rich or greasy foods.

Your tenacious constitution will probably keep you free of major physical ills until about age thirty. After that, a neglect of the rules of physical hygiene will catch up with you, and your intense mental and nervous activity will act upon your natural weaknesses to a serious degree. You need frequent rest periods in your daily work, especially if your work is mental or creative; an atmosphere of calm and harmony is essential to your physical health, and you must keep your bodily functions in smooth and regular working order. You can't run at top speed all your life without paying for it.

YOUR BIRTHRIGHT OF HEALTH

YOUR LIBRA BODY

Though you probably appear to be delicate, even frail, yet you have an extraordinarily sound constitution, with strong powers of endurance and recuperation.

Libra rules the loins, kidneys, generative organs, lumbar region, and the spinal cord. Avoid overly violent exercise, especially that which involves a strain on the back. There is some inclination to kidney ailments, strains, ruptures of vital organs, tumors, and in women to ovarian cysts.

Your character gives rise to few health hazards. Your fine sense of balance and discrimination is a strong protection against excess. While you enjoy good food and drink, and are perhaps more amorous than most of the Signs, you usually manage to keep yourself under control. If the negative side of your nature is developed, however, some weaknesses will flow from your sensitiveness, nervousness, and tendency to worry. Don't let yourself become a hypochondriac, as too many Libras do; you've a good sound body, and only the normal hazards. Your susceptibility to accident is less than normal.

YOUR SCORPIO BODY

Scorpio rules the bladder, groin, the reproductive organs, and to some extent the bloodstream. The latter implies a weakness to eruptions of the skin, and demands caution that any breaking of the skin through accident receive prompt antiseptic treatment. You will find that you do not heal rapidly when cut or bruised. Your doctor will see that you are carefully built up before you undergo any operation and you should follow his orders implicitly, for he knows your danger. There is a related danger to you in ulcerated or infected teeth, infections of the eyes and ears, and in mastoids.

Your constitution is excellent, and your powers of recuperation frequently amazing. But either avoid the overly sedentary life, or balance it with exercise, because of your tendency to ailments involving the circulation. In character, you are very highly sexed; your susceptibility to disease or deterioration of the reproductive organs is frequently aggravated by your inclination to waste your vital forces. Avoid exposure to venereal disease, because of this special hazard. Combat your liking for over-eating, and observe sane rules of diet.

There is a high accident hazard for you. This applies especially to accidents involving vehicles. Your ruling planet Mars governs accidents, and requires that you be unusually careful concerning sharp instruments and explosives; during afflicted cycles, the ultimate in caution will pay you when working around machinery and tools; in automobiles, planes, and in other places of "mechanical" danger.

YOUR SAGITTARIUS BODY

I need say very little to you. Blessed with a sturdy constitution in the beginning, your well-balanced character and intuitive sense of the right thing have made your health hazards less than normal.

Sagittarius rules the thighs. Check up promptly on symptoms which might indicate gout, sciatica, and other ailments of the thighs and hips. Women, by the way, should avoid over-strenuous reducing methods in these regions.

In childhood, there is a tendency toward fevers, chest colds, and bronchial disturbances. You will in all likelihood grow out of this, an expectation which also applies to the susceptibility to disturbances concerning the thyroid and adrenal glands.

There is some inclination to deafness and related afflictions of the ear and aural cavities. Great caution should be taken to avoid ear infections, and the entrance of water and foreign bodies. In the event that heredity has warped your normal Sagittarian "balance," cultivate that moderation which the stars tried to give you. The most common causes of early death in this Sign are apoplexy, paralysis and brain tumor—all in some measure the logical result of excess.

YOUR CAPRICORN BODY

Capricorn tends to a long life and a pretty healthy one. The end, when it comes, is apt to be sudden.

This Sign rules the knees. Beside the usual caution against accidents to this region, care must be taken to avoid rheumatic inflammations. In time of illness, or threatened illness, look to the digestive tract and the function of elimination.

Your nature makes you inclined to dwell on your troubles; and of course dwelling on them merely makes them worse. Perhaps your worst danger comes from your moody, sometimes black and depressed, nature; never resort, as too many Capricorn subjects have, to the artificial buoyancy of liquor and drugs. Not only are you unable to keep such habits under control, but they tend to eat into your character as well as your body.

Saturn inclines you to some extent to diseases involving the lungs, and to malignant growths. I don't want you to become one of these persons who cries "cancer!" at every lump, but I do say that a frequent check-up by a competent physician, with special regard to this susceptibility, is a very good thing. This applies especially if the same tendencies exist in other members of your family.

YOUR BIRTHRIGHT OF HEALTH

Aquarius rules the ankles, legs, teeth, and the circulation of the blood. Your hazards are largely those which come from poor circulation and corrupt blood, particularly rheumatism and rheumatic infections.

Whenever you seem to tire too easily or suffer from insomnia, check with your doctor. Your greatest danger comes from infection, often from poisons originating in bad teeth or tonsils. Don't neglect seemingly harmless cuts or bruises, and avoid malarial climates. Due to your probable poor circulation, you may often feel cold when others are comfortable; you must guard against exposure to low temperature, and take prompt care of chills. The rulership of Aquarius probably burdens you with that plebeian curse, cold feet; keep them warm, in spite of ridicule.

Uranus, your ruling planet, is capable of violent upheavals; sometimes accidents, more often sudden and unexpected illness. Naturally, your greatest accident hazard is to the legs and ankles. Though not brawny in build, your constitution is tenacious and able to withstand most of life's bitterest blows. Keep it that way by overcoming your characteristic tendency to physical inertia; you need plenty of exercise, which you won't take from choice.

It may cheer you to know that if you have suffered at one time of your life from a serious illness, the probabilities are strongly against another serious case —not only of the original ailment, but of any other.

YOUR PISCES BODY

This is a pleasant Sign with which to end our chapter. Pisces is blessed with naturally good health, tends to a very long life, and seldom knows bodily deterioration until well past age 70. You will probably always look younger than your actual years, and feel younger, too.

Your heart is strong and so is your digestive system; both will stand much abuse—though this isn't a suggestion that you abuse them. As a matter of fact, your liking for rich foods, sugar, and condiments often irritates the membranes of the body and causes minor inflammations and congestions of the stomach, kidneys, bladder and liver. Most of your illnesses will be avoidable, and you will have only yourself to blame for poor health.

Pisces rules the feet, and also rules the body fluids. This last, under severe affliction, produces such ailments as dropsy, and disorders of the gall bladder, kidney, and spleen. You must protect yourself against colds, which are too apt with you to cause trouble in the chest and intestines. Occasionally this Sign shows a weakness for over-indulgence in alcohol or drugs. Needless to say, a submission to such an appetite will automatically discard the star-given protection of your naturally superb health.

Just one final caution, which is only indirectly related to the subject in hand. Don't bore other people with long, detailed accounts of your minor illnesses. You won't die of your cough, but they are apt to die of the boredom you induce.

EPILOGUE

THE EGO AND YOUR DESTINY

NO matter in what realm you choose to express your Star-given talents you must be willing to spend a great deal of time in self-analysis and study of your hidden possibilities. All the twelve signs of the Zodiac have been given a definite and clear-cut destiny. There is a purpose in living; and upon investigation you will find that life is not a haphazard, hit-or-miss proposition, but a well-defined pattern that expresses itself in twelve concrete manifestations of Spiritual Ego, through the twelve individual signs of the Zodiac.

As I have told you, heredity, education and environment play a great part in the life of each person, but that indelible stamp placed upon the Ego at the time of YOUR birth remains throughout life, and inclines you to experiences that make you the man or woman you are. That Ego is the expression of your personality to the outer world. It can be a coarse, crude person that the world sees, one with base physical appetites and ambitions; or it can be a fine, noble individual with the highest attributes of man fully developed, expressing that Spiritual consciousness which can elevate you to the supreme heights of immortality.

That Ego, which is You, is fed by your numerous emotional and physical experiences in life. Without this fully developed Ego you cannot go on to your true goal in life; but with a full understanding of the mysterious flow of current which motivates your mind and body, this Ego can become highly sensitized, well developed, and socially conscious of Man's eventual great destiny.

It is this Cosmic Consciousness that seeks to express itself through all the twelve signs of the Zodiac in the individual Egos which are represented by you and me. Each of these twelve elements is essential to the full expression of earthly life, so that no Sign is better than another, and no Sign is really bad, in any sense. To attain this spiritual understanding of Astrology is to give a fuller sense of meaning and beauty to life and its experiences.

You are You because you have a destiny to fulfill; your Ego is as it is because at the time of your birth you absorbed a set of vibrations from the Planets which ordain you to fulfill a definite Destiny. Had you been born in another Sign, your expression of Ego would have been another of those twelve facets, which are the twelve signs of the Zodiac.

THE EGO AND YOUR DESTINY

These twelve Signs of the Zodiac might easily be likened to a diamond. With each turn of the brilliant gem, a new combination of colors flash forth; yours might be the scorching, fiery rays of tempestuousness, emotionalism, and impulsiveness. That is, perhaps, the stamp of your Ego, but turn the Zodiacal gem in another direction, and we have the chilling blue-green rays of the reserved, cold, unemotional and unresponsive Ego. Turn it in still another direction, and ice melts into fire, until the two merge into a glorious fusion of pale orchid, pastel blues and greys.

In such a manner do the individual Egos in the twelve fundamental types of humanity merge, and mingle one with the other. They tend to fuse and combine their Egos, thus to produce the millions of strange and mystifying combinations with which we are familiar in life. People are never the same; Egos are always complemented by those of the parents, and the various life experiences tend to produce an intensification of natural qualities absorbed from our birth signs, or those qualities are modified and lessened.

It is this play of vibratory force upon the individual Egos that causes us to aspire, each and every one, to an ultimate great Destiny. From the lowliest beggar on the city pavements to the most arrogant Dictator sheltered by his picked Guard, humanity is seeking to express his Ego; to find the great Spiritual Goal that keeps men alive and hoping. Some find it, others do not.

The purpose and whole point of living is lost upon the vision of many persons. But these whose eyes are illuminated by the awakened Cosmic Consciousness, these who seek the Spiritual message inscribed in fiery pinpoints of light in the heavens; these are the elect, they are the ones for whom life reserves its greatest blessings; the stars lead them to Soul searching, exploration of the Ego, and through all the numerous vicissitudes of life they gradually are led by the still small voice within them to the blissful walls of Nirvana.

LVIN POWERS SELF-IMPROVEMENT LIBRARY

ASTROLOGY

TROLOGY: HOW TO CHART YOUR HOROSCOPE *Max Heindel* 5.00
TROLOGY AND SEXUAL ANALYSIS *Morris C. Goodman* 7.00
TROLOGY AND YOU *Carroll Righter* 5.00
TROLOGY MADE EASY *Astarte* 7.00
TROLOGY, ROMANCE, YOU AND THE STARS *Anthony Norvell* 10.00
WORLD OF ASTROLOGY *Sydney Omarr* 7.00
OUGHT DIAL *Sydney Omarr* 7.00
AT THE STARS REVEAL ABOUT THE MEN IN YOUR LIFE *Thelma White* 3.00

BRIDGE

IDGE BIDDING MADE EASY *Edwin B. Kantar* 10.00
IDGE CONVENTIONS *Edwin B. Kantar* 10.00
MPETITIVE BIDDING IN MODERN BRIDGE *Edgar Kaplan* 7.00
FENSIVE BRIDGE PLAY COMPLETE *Edwin B. Kantar* 20.00
MESMAN BRIDGE—PLAY BETTER WITH KANTAR *Edwin B. Kantar* 7.00
W TO IMPROVE YOUR BRIDGE *Alfred Sheinwold* 7.00
PROVING YOUR BIDDING SKILLS *Edwin B. Kantar* 7.00
RODUCTION TO DECLARER'S PLAY *Edwin B. Kantar* 7.00
RODUCTION TO DEFENDER'S PLAY *Edwin B. Kantar* 7.00
NTAR FOR THE DEFENSE *Edwin B. Kantar* 7.00
NTAR FOR THE DEFENSE VOLUME 2 *Edwin B. Kantar* 7.00
ST YOUR BRIDGE PLAY *Edwin B. Kantar* 7.00
LUME 2—TEST YOUR BRIDGE PLAY *Edwin B. Kantar* 10.00
NNING DECLARER PLAY *Dorothy Hayden Truscott* 10.00

BUSINESS, STUDY & REFERENCE

AINSTORMING *Charles Clark* 10.00
NVERSATION MADE EASY *Elliot Russell* 5.00
AM SECRET *Dennis B. Jackson* 5.00
IT BOOK *Arthur Symons* 2.00
W TO DEVELOP A BETTER SPEAKING VOICE *M. Hellier* 5.00
W TO SAVE 50% ON GAS & CAR EXPENSES *Ken Stansbie* 5.00
W TO SELF-PUBLISH YOUR BOOK & MAKE IT A BEST SELLER *Melvin Powers* .. 20.00
REASE YOUR LEARNING POWER *Geoffrey A. Dudley* 5.00
ACTICAL GUIDE TO BETTER CONCENTRATION *Melvin Powers* 5.00
BLIC SPEAKING MADE EASY *Thomas Montalbo* 10.00
AYS TO FASTER READING *William S. Schaill* 7.00
NGWRITERS' RHYMING DICTIONARY *Jane Shaw Whitfield* 10.00
ELLING MADE EASY *Lester D. Basch & Dr. Milton Finkelstein* 3.00
JDENT'S GUIDE TO BETTER GRADES *J. A. Rickard* 3.00
ST YOURSELF—FIND YOUR HIDDEN TALENT *Jack Shafer* 3.00
JR WILL & WHAT TO DO ABOUT IT *Attorney Samuel G. Kling* 7.00

CALLIGRAPHY

VANCED CALLIGRAPHY *Katherine Jeffares* 7.00
LLIGRAPHY—THE ART OF BEAUTIFUL WRITING *Katherine Jeffares* 7.00
LLIGRAPHY FOR FUN & PROFIT *Anne Leptich & Jacque Evans* 7.00
LLIGRAPHY MADE EASY *Tina Serafini* 7.00

CHESS & CHECKERS

GINNER'S GUIDE TO WINNING CHESS *Fred Reinfeld* 7.00
ESS IN TEN EASY LESSONS *Larry Evans* 10.00
ESS MADE EASY *Milton L. Hanauer* 5.00
ESS PROBLEMS FOR BEGINNERS *Edited by Fred Reinfeld* 5.00

____ CHESS TACTICS FOR BEGINNERS *Edited by Fred Reinfeld* ....
____ HOW TO WIN AT CHECKERS *Fred Reinfeld* ....
____ 1001 BRILLIANT WAYS TO CHECKMATE *Fred Reinfeld* ....
____ 1001 WINNING CHESS SACRIFICES & COMBINATIONS *Fred Reinfeld* ....

COOKERY & HERBS

____ CULPEPER'S HERBAL REMEDIES *Dr. Nicholas Culpeper* ....
____ FAST GOURMET COOKBOOK *Poppy Cannon* ....
____ HEALING POWER OF HERBS *May Bethel* ....
____ HEALING POWER OF NATURAL FOODS *May Bethel* ....
____ HERBS FOR HEALTH—HOW TO GROW & USE THEM *Louise Evans Doole* ....
____ HOME GARDEN COOKBOOK—DELICIOUS NATURAL FOOD RECIPES *Ken Kraft* ...
____ MEATLESS MEAL GUIDE *Tomi Ryan & James H. Ryan, M.D.* ....
____ VEGETABLE GARDENING FOR BEGINNERS *Hugh Wiberg* ....
____ VEGETABLES FOR TODAY'S GARDENS *R. Milton Carleton* ....
____ VEGETARIAN COOKERY *Janet Walker* ....
____ VEGETARIAN COOKING MADE EASY & DELECTABLE *Veronica Vezza* ....
____ VEGETARIAN DELIGHTS—A HAPPY COOKBOOK FOR HEALTH *K. R. Mehta* ....

GAMBLING & POKER

____ HOW TO WIN AT POKER *Terence Reese & Anthony T. Watkins* ....
____ SCARNE ON DICE *John Scarne* ....
____ WINNING AT CRAPS *Dr. Lloyd T. Commins* ....
____ WINNING AT GIN *Chester Wander & Cy Rice* ....
____ WINNING AT POKER—AN EXPERT'S GUIDE *John Archer* ....
____ WINNING AT 21—AN EXPERT'S GUIDE *John Archer* ....
____ WINNING POKER SYSTEMS *Norman Zadeh* ....

HEALTH

____ BEE POLLEN *Lynda Lyngheim & Jack Scagnetti* ....
____ COPING WITH ALZHEIMER'S *Rose Oliver, Ph.D. & Francis Bock, Ph.D.* ....
____ DR. LINDNER'S POINT SYSTEM FOOD PROGRAM *Peter G. Lindner, M.D.* ....
____ HELP YOURSELF TO BETTER SIGHT *Margaret Darst Corbett* ....
____ HOW YOU CAN STOP SMOKING PERMANENTLY *Ernest Caldwell* ....
____ MIND OVER PLATTER *Peter G. Lindner, M.D.* ....
____ NATURE'S WAY TO NUTRITION & VIBRANT HEALTH *Robert J. Scrutton* ....
____ NEW CARBOHYDRATE DIET COUNTER *Patti Lopez-Pereira* ....
____ REFLEXOLOGY *Dr. Maybelle Segal* ....
____ REFLEXOLOGY FOR GOOD HEALTH *Anna Kaye & Don C. Matchan* ....
____ 30 DAYS TO BEAUTIFUL LEGS *Dr. Marc Selner* ....
____ WONDER WITHIN *Thomas F. Coyle, M.D.* ....
____ YOU CAN LEARN TO RELAX *Dr. Samuel Gutwirth* ....

HOBBIES

____ BEACHCOMBING FOR BEGINNERS *Norman Hickin* ....
____ BLACKSTONE'S MODERN CARD TRICKS *Harry Blackstone* ....
____ BLACKSTONE'S SECRETS OF MAGIC *Harry Blackstone* ....
____ COIN COLLECTING FOR BEGINNERS *Burton Hobson & Fred Reinfeld* ....
____ ENTERTAINING WITH ESP *Tony 'Doc' Shiels* ....
____ 400 FASCINATING MAGIC TRICKS YOU CAN DO *Howard Thurston* ....
____ HOW I TURN JUNK INTO FUN AND PROFIT *Sari* ....
____ HOW TO WRITE A HIT SONG & SELL IT *Tommy Boyce* ....
____ MAGIC FOR ALL AGES *Walter Gibson* ....
____ STAMP COLLECTING FOR BEGINNERS *Burton Hobson* ....

HORSE PLAYER'S WINNING GUIDES

ETTING HORSES TO WIN *Les Conklin*	7.00
LIMINATE THE LOSERS *Bob McKnight*	5.00
OW TO PICK WINNING HORSES *Bob McKnight*	5.00
OW TO WIN AT THE RACES *Sam (The Genius) Lewin*	5.00
OW YOU CAN BEAT THE RACES *Jack Kavanagh*	5.00
AKING MONEY AT THE RACES *David Barr*	5.00
AYDAY AT THE RACES *Les Conklin*	7.00
MART HANDICAPPING MADE EASY *William Bauman*	5.00
UCCESS AT THE HARNESS RACES *Barry Meadow*	7.00

HUMOR

OW TO FLATTEN YOUR TUSH *Coach Marge Reardon*	2.00
OKE TELLER'S HANDBOOK *Bob Orben*	7.00
OKES FOR ALL OCCASIONS *Al Schock*	5.00
000 NEW LAUGHS FOR SPEAKERS *Bob Orben*	7.00
400 JOKES TO BRIGHTEN YOUR SPEECHES *Robert Orben*	7.00
500 JOKES TO START 'EM LAUGHING *Bob Orben*	10.00

HYPNOTISM

HILDBIRTH WITH HYPNOSIS *William S. Kroger, M.D.*	5.00
OW TO SOLVE YOUR SEX PROBLEMS WITH SELF-HYPNOSIS *Frank S. Caprio, M.D.*	5.00
OW TO STOP SMOKING THRU SELF-HYPNOSIS *Leslie M. LeCron*	3.00
OW YOU CAN BOWL BETTER USING SELF-HYPNOSIS *Jack Heise*	7.00
OW YOU CAN PLAY BETTER GOLF USING SELF-HYPNOSIS *Jack Heise*	3.00
YPNOSIS AND SELF-HYPNOSIS *Bernard Hollander, M.D.*	7.00
YPNOTISM *(Originally published in 1893) Carl Sextus*	5.00
YPNOTISM MADE EASY *Dr. Ralph Winn*	7.00
YPNOTISM MADE PRACTICAL *Louis Orton*	5.00
YPNOTISM REVEALED *Melvin Powers*	3.00
YPNOTISM TODAY *Leslie LeCron and Jean Bordeaux, Ph.D.*	5.00
ODERN HYPNOSIS *Lesley Kuhn & Salvatore Russo, Ph.D.*	5.00
EW CONCEPTS OF HYPNOSIS *Bernard C. Gindes, M.D.*	10.00
EW SELF-HYPNOSIS *Paul Adams*	10.00
OST-HYPNOTIC INSTRUCTIONS—SUGGESTIONS FOR THERAPY *Arnold Furst*	10.00
RACTICAL GUIDE TO SELF-HYPNOSIS *Melvin Powers*	5.00
RACTICAL HYPNOTISM *Philip Magonet, M.D.*	3.00
CRETS OF HYPNOTISM *S. J. Van Pelt, M.D.*	5.00
LF-HYPNOSIS—A CONDITIONED-RESPONSE TECHNIQUE *Laurence Sparks*	7.00
LF-HYPNOSIS—ITS THEORY, TECHNIQUE & APPLICATION *Melvin Powers*	3.00
ERAPY THROUGH HYPNOSIS *Edited by Raphael H. Rhodes*	5.00

JUDAICA

RVICE OF THE HEART *Evelyn Garfiel, Ph.D.*	10.00
ORY OF ISRAEL IN COINS *Jean & Maurice Gould*	2.00
ORY OF ISRAEL IN STAMPS *Maxim & Gabriel Shamir*	1.00
NGUE OF THE PROPHETS *Robert St. John*	10.00

JUST FOR WOMEN

OSMOPOLITAN'S GUIDE TO MARVELOUS MEN Foreword by *Helen Gurley Brown*	3.00
OSMOPOLITAN'S HANG-UP HANDBOOK Foreword by *Helen Gurley Brown*	4.00
OSMOPOLITAN'S LOVE BOOK—A GUIDE TO ECSTASY IN BED	7.00
OSMOPOLITAN'S NEW ETIQUETTE GUIDE Foreword by *Helen Gurley Brown*	4.00
M A COMPLEAT WOMAN *Doris Hagopian & Karen O'Connor Sweeney*	3.00
ST FOR WOMEN—A GUIDE TO THE FEMALE BODY *Richard E. Sand, M.D.*	5.00
W APPROACHES TO SEX IN MARRIAGE *John E. Eichenlaub, M.D.*	3.00
XUALLY ADEQUATE FEMALE *Frank S. Caprio, M.D.*	3.00
XUALLY FULFILLED WOMAN *Dr. Rachel Copelan*	5.00

MARRIAGE, SEX & PARENTHOOD

___ ABILITY TO LOVE *Dr. Allan Fromme* . . . .

___ GUIDE TO SUCCESSFUL MARRIAGE *Drs. Albert Ellis & Robert Harper* . . . .

___ HOW TO RAISE AN EMOTIONALLY HEALTHY, HAPPY CHILD *Albert Ellis, Ph.D.* . . . .

___ PARENT SURVIVAL TRAINING *Marvin Silverman, Ed.D. & David Lustig, Ph.D.* . . . . . .

___ SEX WITHOUT GUILT *Albert Ellis, Ph.D.* . . . .

___ SEXUALLY ADEQUATE MALE *Frank S. Caprio, M.D.* . . . .

___ SEXUALLY FULFILLED MAN *Dr. Rachel Copelan* . . . .

___ STAYING IN LOVE *Dr. Norton F. Kristy* . . . .

MELVIN POWERS' MAIL ORDER LIBRARY

___ HOW TO GET RICH IN MAIL ORDER *Melvin Powers* . . . .

___ HOW TO SELF-PUBLISH YOUR BOOK & MAKE IT A BEST SELLER *Melvin Powers* .

___ HOW TO WRITE A GOOD ADVERTISEMENT *Victor O. Schwab* . . . .

___ MAIL ORDER MADE EASY *J. Frank Brumbaugh* . . . .

METAPHYSICS & OCCULT

___ CONCENTRATION—A GUIDE TO MENTAL MASTERY *Mouni Sadhu* . . . .

___ EXTRA-TERRESTRIAL INTELLIGENCE—THE FIRST ENCOUNTER . . . .

___ FORTUNE TELLING WITH CARDS *P. Foli* . . . .

___ HOW TO INTERPRET DREAMS, OMENS & FORTUNE TELLING SIGNS *Gettings* . .

___ HOW TO UNDERSTAND YOUR DREAMS *Geoffrey A. Dudley* . . . .

___ MAGICIAN—HIS TRAINING AND WORK *W. E. Butler* . . . .

___ MEDITATION *Mouni Sadhu* . . . .

___ MODERN NUMEROLOGY *Morris C. Goodman* . . . .

___ NUMEROLOGY—ITS FACTS AND SECRETS *Ariel Yvon Taylor* . . . .

___ NUMEROLOGY MADE EASY *W. Mykian* . . . .

___ PALMISTRY MADE EASY *Fred Gettings* . . . .

___ PALMISTRY MADE PRACTICAL *Elizabeth Daniels Squire* . . . .

___ PROPHECY IN OUR TIME *Martin Ebon* . . . .

___ SUPERSTITION—ARE YOU SUPERSTITIOUS? *Eric Maple* . . . .

___ TAROT *Mouni Sadhu* . . . .

___ TAROT OF THE BOHEMIANS *Papus* . . . .

___ WAYS TO SELF-REALIZATION *Mouni Sadhu* . . . .

___ WITCHCRAFT, MAGIC & OCCULTISM—A FASCINATING HISTORY *W. B. Crow* . . . .

___ WITCHCRAFT—THE SIXTH SENSE *Justine Glass* . . . .

RECOVERY

___ KNIGHT IN RUSTY ARMOR *Robert Fisher* . . . .

___ KNIGHT IN RUSTY ARMOR *Robert Fisher (Hard cover edition)* . . . .

___ KNIGHTS WITHOUT ARMOR *Aaron R. Kipnis, Ph.D. (Hard cover edition)* . . . .

SELF-HELP & INSPIRATIONAL

___ CHARISMA—HOW TO GET "THAT SPECIAL MAGIC" *Marcia Grad* . . . .

___ DAILY POWER FOR JOYFUL LIVING *Dr. Donald Curtis* . . . .

___ DYNAMIC THINKING *Melvin Powers* . . . .

___ GREATEST POWER IN THE UNIVERSE *U. S. Andersen* . . . .

___ GROW RICH WHILE YOU SLEEP *Ben Sweetland* . . . .

___ GROW RICH WITH YOUR MILLION DOLLAR MIND *Brian Adams* . . . .

___ GROWTH THROUGH REASON *Albert Ellis, Ph.D.* . . . .

___ GUIDE TO PERSONAL HAPPINESS *Albert Ellis, Ph.D. & Irving Becker, Ed.D.* . . . . . .

___ HANDWRITING ANALYSIS MADE EASY *John Marley* . . . .

___ HANDWRITING TELLS *Nadya Olyanova* . . . .

___ HOW TO ATTRACT GOOD LUCK *A.H.Z. Carr* . . . .

___ HOW TO DEVELOP A WINNING PERSONALITY *Martin Panzer* . . . .

___ HOW TO DEVELOP AN EXCEPTIONAL MEMORY *Young & Gibson* . . . .

___ HOW TO LIVE WITH A NEUROTIC *Albert Ellis, Ph.D.* . . . .

___ HOW TO OVERCOME YOUR FEARS *M. P. Leahy, M.D.* . . . .

___ HOW TO SUCCEED *Brian Adams* . . . .

HUMAN PROBLEMS & HOW TO SOLVE THEM *Dr. Donald Curtis* 5.00
I CAN *Ben Sweetland* 8.00
I WILL *Ben Sweetland* 10.00
KNIGHT IN RUSTY ARMOR *Robert Fisher* 5.00
KNIGHT IN RUSTY ARMOR *Robert Fisher (Hard cover edition)* 10.00
LEFT-HANDED PEOPLE *Michael Barsley* 5.00
MAGIC IN YOUR MIND *U.S. Andersen* 10.00
MAGIC OF THINKING SUCCESS *Dr. David J. Schwartz* 8.00
MAGIC POWER OF YOUR MIND *Walter M. Germain* 7.00
MENTAL POWER THROUGH SLEEP SUGGESTION *Melvin Powers* 3.00
NEVER UNDERESTIMATE THE SELLING POWER OF A WOMAN *Dottie Walters*..... 7.00
NEW GUIDE TO RATIONAL LIVING *Albert Ellis, Ph.D. & R. Harper, Ph.D.* 10.00
PSYCHO-CYBERNETICS *Maxwell Maltz, M.D.* 7.00
PSYCHOLOGY OF HANDWRITING *Nadya Olyanova* 7.00
SALES CYBERNETICS *Brian Adams* 10.00
SCIENCE OF MIND IN DAILY LIVING *Dr. Donald Curtis* 7.00
SECRET OF SECRETS *U.S. Andersen* 7.00
SECRET POWER OF THE PYRAMIDS *U. S. Andersen* 7.00
SELF-THERAPY FOR THE STUTTERER *Malcolm Frazer* 3.00
SUCCESS-CYBERNETICS *U. S. Andersen* 7.00
10 DAYS TO A GREAT NEW LIFE *William E. Edwards* 3.00
THINK AND GROW RICH *Napoleon Hill* 8.00
THINK LIKE A WINNER *Dr. Walter Doyle Staples* 10.00
THREE MAGIC WORDS *U. S. Andersen* 10.00
TREASURY OF COMFORT *Edited by Rabbi Sidney Greenberg* 10.00
TREASURY OF THE ART OF LIVING *Sidney S. Greenberg* 7.00
WHAT YOUR HANDWRITING REVEALS *Albert E. Hughes* 4.00
WONDER WITHIN *Thomas F. Coyle, M.D.* 10.00
YOUR SUBCONSCIOUS POWER *Charles M. Simmons* 7.00
YOUR THOUGHTS CAN CHANGE YOUR LIFE *Dr. Donald Curtis*................ 7.00

SPORTS

BILLIARDS—POCKET • CAROM • THREE CUSHION *Clive Cottingham, Jr.* 7.00
COMPLETE GUIDE TO FISHING *Vlad Evanoff* 2.00
HOW TO IMPROVE YOUR RACQUETBALL *Lubarsky, Kaufman & Scagnetti* 5.00
HOW TO WIN AT POCKET BILLIARDS *Edward D. Knuchell* 10.00
JOY OF WALKING *Jack Scagnetti* 3.00
LEARNING & TEACHING SOCCER SKILLS *Eric Worthington* 3.00
RACQUETBALL FOR WOMEN *Toni Hudson, Jack Scagnetti & Vince Rondone* 3.00
SECRET OF BOWLING STRIKES *Dawson Taylor* 5.00
SOCCER—THE GAME & HOW TO PLAY IT *Gary Rosenthal* 7.00
STARTING SOCCER *Edward F. Dolan, Jr.* 3.00

TENNIS LOVER'S LIBRARY

HOW TO BEAT BETTER TENNIS PLAYERS *Loring Fiske* 4.00
PSYCH YOURSELF TO BETTER TENNIS *Dr. Walter A. Luszki* 2.00
TENNIS FOR BEGINNERS *Dr. H. A. Murray* 2.00
TENNIS MADE EASY *Joel Brecheen* 5.00
WEEKEND TENNIS—HOW TO HAVE FUN & WIN AT THE SAME TIME *Bill Talbert* ... 3.00

WILSHIRE PET LIBRARY

DOG TRAINING MADE EASY & FUN *John W. Kellogg* 5.00
HOW TO BRING UP YOUR PET DOG *Kurt Unkelbach* 2.00
HOW TO RAISE & TRAIN YOUR PUPPY *Jeff Griffen* 5.00

Books listed above can be obtained from your book dealer or directly from Melvin Powers. When ordering, please remit $2.00 postage for the first book and $1.00 for each additional book.

Melvin Powers
12015 Sherman Road, No. Hollywood, California 91605